LEADERSHIP

for

LANDLORDS

Property Leadership Handbook

for the

Modern Landlord

ANTHONY RUSSELL

LEADERSHIP FOR LANDLORDS

PROPERTY LEADERSHIP HANDBOOK FOR THE MODERN LANDLORD

ANTHONY RUSSELL

ISBN: 978-0-578-92666-7 (paperback)

CONTENTS

I dedicate this book to my wife, who is my best friend, and my son.

Without my wife's constant honesty, love and guidance, I wouldn't have the love for nature and life the way I do today.

Without my son, I wouldn't have the constant motivation to be better than I am.

Thank you both.

"...But lest some unlucky event should happen unfavorable to my reputation, I beg it may be remembered by every gentleman in the room that I, this day, declare with the utmost sincerity, I do not think myself equal to the command I am honored with..."

George Washington's speech accepting his appointment as Commander of the Continental Army, June 16th, 1775

INTRODUCTION

Anyone who has spent time in the United States Military knows that we have some of the strongest leaders in the world. That's not due to any coincidence or string of luck. It is through a deliberate series of trials and training that the men and women of the US Military develop the skills for extraordinary leadership. I served as an Army Military Police Officer on active duty for five years. During that time, I did 15 months in Baquba, Iraq where I helped train Iraqi Police, set up Iraqi Police stations, and ran route security. I also spent time on a quick response team. I did dismounted patrols throughout the city of Baquba, and I was both a 50-caliber machine gunner on top of an M1114 Humvee and a driver of Humvees and Armored Security Vehicles.

When I got back from Iraq, I was promoted to Sergeant, and attended the four-week Warrior Leadership Course at Fort Lewis. All these experiences honed my skills and mind to make me a hardened leader. I learned quickly to remove emotion from decisions and to always put the people below me first. When I left the Army, I knew that I would always carry those skills with me and apply them to be the best at whatever I ended up doing, wherever I ended up working.

About a decade ago, I was freshly divorced, with almost no money to my name, no job, and a young child who needed me to provide for him. I was discouraged but far from hopeless. The military had woken the never-quit attitude in me. I just needed to unleash it.

Soon enough, I did.

Five short years later, I achieved financial independence through real estate investing with rock-solid fundamentals. By reading this book and applying the knowledge in it, you'll be able to do the same.

Some of this book's content might seem controversial. I know plenty of property owners that would dispute much of what I think and how I run my rentals. That said, I'm successful, and a lot of them aren't. That is due in large part to the processes that I've put in place as a leader in my business.

The ethics by which I do things keep my buildings profitable, but more importantly, they keep the people in them happy. And you know what? Here's the first lesson for you, are you ready for it? If you treat all of your tenants like they're the customer and not like warm bodies to pay you rent, you'll be successful too. Shocking, right? I know that doesn't seem like a radical idea, but I can't tell you how many horror stories I've heard from tenants over the years about former landlords. Treating people right should be your cornerstone. The money will follow.

One final note before you start this book: remember that great leaders eat last. You may not understand this mentality or phrase just yet, but if you keep reading, you soon will. At first, you may think this a poor way to run a business. I'm here to tell you, though, that if you want to be a great leader, you'll put the welfare of everyone else before yourself. You'll jump at the opportunity to take care of others, and you'll cringe at the idea of taking advantage of those that trust you. If you want to be the type of leader that milks their tenants for everything without giving back, then close this book now and get a refund. I can't help you. Honestly, I don't want to. I'm not here to empower douchebags. I'm here to help people—leaders—run their rentals the right way. The profitable way.

CHAPTER 1

LAND LEADERSHIP

"Serving others prepares you to lead others." — *Jim George*

THOSE WHO KNEW me in school would have been hard-pressed to find a single leadership bone in my body. I played sports but wasn't really athletic. I was the first chair in the Jazz, Marching, and Concert band, but I never really took charge of the section. I even had many part-time micro-companies that I started to make extra cash, but most of them went under as quickly as they formed.

Those I meet today assume I've always been a leader. They think that I had a privileged upbringing, that my parents gave me money to start my rental business or that I used my relationship with them to open doors faster. Nothing could be further from the truth, though.

When I was growing up, my parents had nothing. In

fact, I even remember them going bankrupt at one point. We relied on low-income stores like Aldis and Big Lots. And oh, how I despised my parents for it. Like many entitled kids, I had no idea how the real world worked at the time. I'm pretty thankful now for this experience. Growing up in a very frugal household meant that I needed to be resourceful to get the things I wanted in life. So, I guess people do have a reason to be jealous of my upbringing. If it weren't for those lessons in frugality from my parents, I probably wouldn't have the life skills I needed to make it through the lean times without going deep into debt.

My parents taught me that working hard and saving was the best way to get ahead. They also taught me that if you really want something, you'll find a way to get it. So, my childhood was filled with garage sales, mowing lawns, pulling weeds, raking leaves, and so on. I remember times that I would even buy candy and sell it door to door.

These days, someone would have a conniption if they saw an 8-12-year-old doing those things, but that's how it was when I was growing up. I learned very early that hard work and a little hustle could make a ton of money.

The first real entrepreneurial pursuit I remember starting was my lawn mowing business. Growing up in the nineties was great. Consumer technology was really taking off. You could buy all types of neat gizmos. At that time, cell phones were the new big thing. They were just flip phones, with no internet, only text and talking. They were also super expensive to operate regularly. I remember it being around $1.50 per minute to talk, and when you sent text messages, they took a fraction of your minutes.

I remember that all my friends had cell phones and I really wanted one. But my friends also had wealthy parents who bought the phones for them. They rarely, if ever, had to work for things like this. Now as I said, my parents didn't have a ton of money. There was no way they were going to spring for a cell phone, let alone monthly minutes for me. If I wanted it, I was going to have to work for it. So naturally, I hand drew some flyers and started handing them out around the neighborhood.

At first, it was a slow start, just one or two lawns a week at $20 per lawn. This pretty much gave me enough to afford my phone at $50-$100 each month, but then it happened: I started getting more work than I could handle. Before I knew it, I was making well over $200 a week mowing lawns. Each lawn took me around 30 minutes to complete, and I made $20 per property. This means that I was making $200 a week for working just 5 hours. This was my first success going it alone, and it opened my eyes to what many of my peers didn't see. While they were hanging around the mall after school, partying every weekend, and wasting every extra hour on video games, I was discovering what just a bit of drive and some of my free time could do.

This realization set me up for a life of constantly doing the opposite of everyone else. As I got older, noting what everyone else was doing and then doing the opposite became a North Star. This is a principle that I carry with me to this day. What is normal in our world is often dictated by the group, and the group is often irrational, dumb, and motivated by corporations who want their money.

Soon enough, hustles like mowing lawns stopped, and I started working real jobs. My first was at Hallmark, where I made $5.10 an hour. I'll never forget that job. It was horrible. On my first day, I was working in the stock room in the back. The stockroom was about eight feet wide with shelves on both sides, floor to ceiling. On these shelves were thousands and thousands of boxes, all of which had long SKU numbers on them. My very first job was to organize this back room, one box at a time, all by myself.

So I began, one box after the next. Hours and hours went by, shift after shift. I spent weeks in this tiny stockroom moving boxes around as we prepared for the holidays.

By December, I had organized most of the stock room. I was excited that I'd done such a great job, and since Christmas was coming soon, I thought maybe I'd get a bonus. My family, like most, had a holiday party coming up and I wanted to get my parents something nice. It would be the first time in my life that I could afford to buy gifts for them, and I was super excited. I'd probably even buy it from Hallmark.

These thoughts ran through my head while I finished up in the stockroom, and I remembered that I had to tell the owner I needed to take off for Christmas Eve and Christmas for my parents' Christmas party. I went out into the main store and found the owner.

I'll never forget the next moment. The owner was kneeling down, stacking those stupid little hummel figures onto a glass display. I took a deep breath.

"Sir, my mom had told me that we had plans for

Christmas, so I needed to make sure that you knew I was going to need to take Christmas Eve and Christmas off."

Without hesitation, he looked up at me and said in an impatient and angry tone.

"Seriously? That's what I hired you for. You're fired, get out of here."

Just like that, after only three months, at the age of fifteen and a half, I had been fired from my first job. I was crushed. I was confused. I didn't know how to process what had just happened. Most importantly, was this going to stay on my permanent record? Would I ever be able to work again?

I had to walk about a mile home, in shame, to tell my mom and dad what had happened. They weren't happy about me losing my job, but they saw it as a good life lesson. Sometimes, bad things happen when you least expect them. This was bad, but they knew I'd recover.

Things went on like that for a while; I got jobs, I lost jobs, nothing spectacular ever really came about from them. I worked as a cook for a few years and even went to a culinary school, but it just wasn't for me. I thought I'd never find my passion or any excitement. That is until I joined the Army.

The Army was certainly a new experience. I didn't know what to expect. If I had known what to expect, like many, I probably wouldn't have joined. The military is funny like that. They suck the romance out of the notion of service really quick, and all you're left with is a 5-year contract and plenty of work to do. The military developed my work ethic for sure. Long days, hard work, cold nights outside, and sleeping in the bush build character.

Experiences like that teach you quickly that you can't quit when things get tough. For the fortunate ones like me, the lessons we absorbed during that time will serve us for the rest of our lives. We'll continue to apply them to whatever we pursue next. My time in the military, though it was difficult, is probably one of the most cherished memories I have at this point in life. The friendships and life lessons were well worth the long days and hard work.

Right from the start, the military grooms leaders. From the moment you step off the cattle car, they drill the core fundamentals of great leadership into you.

- Loyalty
- Duty
- Respect
- Selfless Service
- Honor
- Integrity
- Personal Courage

These are just a few things that make a soldier. Night and day, you live and breathe these values. The military is so focused on making phenomenal leaders right from the start, they've built their principles around it. If you look at the above list again, you'll see it's an acronym. L.D.R.S.H.I.P. These seven Army Core Values, by which every soldier in the Army lives and breathes spell out leadership.

I do mean everyone lives and breathes it, too. If someone in your unit fails to uphold any one of these values, you're all punished together. You live as a team, and you die as a team. There is no room for individuals in a combat unit.

No one comes out of Basic Training a leader, though. Everyone in the military starts as a follower. I think that this is probably one of the biggest things I see people missing today. Everyone wants to give orders and be in charge, but no one wants to take orders and listen first. Before you can lead, you must be able to follow. This is where you gain perspective. When you're a follower, you're able to step back and observe your leader's strategy, their approach to guiding their team, and you can learn from that. I certainly did. In a leadership position, things get more complicated. They will be harder than ever. As a follower, you have only your own job and your wellbeing to consider. When you're a leader, you have that, plus the problems of everyone under you.

You learn that true leadership is more than just barking orders. It's an art. It's a skill that is developed over time. Even natural-born leaders need to learn to hone their talents. There's more to moving troops than being charismatic.

Contrary to what many believe, this is true for landlords as well. Doing the job right requires serious leadership. I know that this may come as a shock to many current landlords, but as a landlord, you ARE a leader.

- You're the captain of the ship.
- You're the President and CEO.
- The buck stops with you
- You're the driving force of success behind your business.

- You decide what will and will not go down in your properties.
- You dictate how leases are written, what contractors you hire or don't hire.
- You handle all the finances, and even at times, you'll have to mediate between tenants.

Yes, if you are in this position and you don't have leadership skills, then woe is you.

It's up to the captain to steer the ship. It's up to the captain to make sure the ship stays upright and that everyone does what they're supposed to.

Your job as captain of your rental business will be to make sure the rent is collected, the mortgage and other bills are paid, and when shit inevitably starts to go sideways, it's your job to fix it.

Believe it or not, your tenants won't do any of this for you. Your tenants aren't going to volunteer to pay to fix things, and they certainly won't pay your mortgage for you. This is the job of the captain.

The nice part about being the captain of the ship is that you get to decide where you go. From port to port, you'll sail. You'll avoid obstacles, and you'll get better as you go. The success or failure of your ship and your crew is squarely on your shoulders. Should you fail, the failure is yours and yours alone.

If you fail, it's YOUR fault.

Let me emphasize this for a moment because it's probably the hardest lesson for everyone to learn.

If your ship crashes into the rocks for ANY REASON, it's you, the captain, your fault.

Not your tenant's fault, not the neighborhood, not the real estate agent, not your cousin Billy Joe, yours.

I can't stress this enough. A huge first step in becoming a great leader is accepting responsibility for everything. If you constantly try and blame others, whether rightfully or not, then you're going to fail.

I know this seems a bit unfair, but it's the truth if you want to succeed. If you don't take responsibility, you'll get caught up in the blame game and you won't do what needs to get done.

Real leaders first take responsibility; then they take action.

Weak leaders are quick to blame others. Weak leaders are often afraid of confrontation, quick to point their finger at others, slow to take action, and love being entitled.

Strong leaders are quick to take responsibility. They're equally as quick to take action to fix problems. They're not afraid to stand up for what is right, and they have enough humility to admit when they're wrong.

I think that this is why I love property management so much. It's an excellent test of one's character. If you can't handle people saying mean things, stuff breaking when you're low on cash, taking calls during Wheel of Fortune, and being ready to list and sell a unit at a moment's notice, then put your money in a low fee index fund and continue being a slave to corporate America, because this job isn't for you.

For those of you that are ready for this life, just know that even for strong leaders, it's still a challenge. That's what makes life fun, though. That's what keeps the job fresh: the never-ending challenges presented to you.

As you go, it gets easier to deal with, but the challenges never stop. One day everything will be fine, and the next day, you're going to have three feet of water in your basement. On the 31st of the month, your tenant will be smiling to your face, and the following day, they're going to be crying to you on the phone about how they don't have enough money to cover their rent because they decided to go out partying the weekend before.

You're always going to have new and exciting challenges to face, especially when you're first starting out. Some of the things you'll see over and over. It'll become easier. Just don't give up.

What makes it doable is keeping your goals in mind, and as a landlord, you are leading everyone towards the joint goal of having and maintaining a hospitable home.

This is a complex and multi-faceted goal, just as leading soldiers to win a battle is. That is why military personnel is supplied with principles to guide them. It provides something to measure one's progress against and serves as a map towards a goal. Fortunately, these guidelines are applicable beyond military life as well. That's why I want to share with you the Noncommissioned Officer's Creed before proceeding with the content of this book.

Since the United States has an all-volunteer military, only about 1% of the population ever serves. What follows are the words that the leaders of the 1% memorize, live, and breathe. If you do the same, you'll pave a path for yourself to join them.

THE NCO CREED

No one is more professional than I. I am a Noncommissioned Officer, a leader of Soldiers. As a Noncommissioned Officer, I realize that I am a member of a time honored corps, which is known as "The Backbone of the Army." I am proud of the Corps of Noncommissioned Officers, and will at all times conduct myself so as to bring credit upon the Corps, the military service, and my country; regardless of the situation in which I find myself. I will not use my grade or position to attain pleasure, profit, or personal safety.

Competence is my watchword. My two basic responsibilities will always be uppermost in my mind: The accomplishment of my mission and the welfare of my Soldiers. I will strive to remain technically and tactically proficient. I am aware of my role as a Noncommissioned Officer, I will fulfill my responsibilities inherent in that role. All Soldiers are entitled to outstanding leadership; I will provide that leadership. I know my Soldiers, and I will always place their needs above my own. I will communicate consistently with my Soldiers, and never leave them uninformed. I will be fair and impartial when recommending both rewards and punishment.

Officers of my unit will have maximum time to accomplish their duties; they will not have to accomplish mine. I will earn their respect and confidence as well as that of my Soldiers. I will be loyal to those with whom I serve; seniors, peers, and subordinates alike. I will exercise initiative by taking appropriate action in the absence of orders. I will not compromise my integrity, nor my moral courage. I will not forget, nor will I allow my comrades to forget that we are professionals, Noncommissioned Officers, leaders!

CHAPTER 2

WEAK LEADERS

"The ear of the leader must ring with the voices of the people."— *Woodrow Wilson*

WHEN PEOPLE ASK me about being a property manager, I often hear

"I don't want to fix toilets at midnight."

My response usually is

"No kidding, me neither."

Honestly, I can't tell you the last time I fixed a toilet at midnight. My tenants don't call me at crazy hours, and the things they do call about are usually minor. That all being said, if someone did call me at midnight and told me that their toilet just exploded off the floor and there was water running everywhere, you bet your ass I'd be there.

You can't choose when things go bad. You can't choose how expensive things will be to fix. What you can choose, though, is how you respond. If you respond with anger, sadness, or anxiety, then once those emotions clear, you're still going to have to fix whatever you were called for. The faster you learn to detach emotion from your rental business, the better off you'll be.

You have to have the correct mindset going into this job. Your mindset as a leader is key. With the wrong mindset, your tenants will not follow you, and you will certainly fail.

With the wrong mindset, you'll also spend months or years blaming other people for failures that will never get resolved.

Remember that one tenant that one time that did that one thing? Yeah, you're still upset about it, and you're still waiting for them to come back to resolve the issue by paying you that $50.00 that they owe you for whatever.

This is a common theme I hear from landlords. They're upset because they even won a judgment in court against a tenant, and that person still hasn't paid a dime.

DON'T BE THIS PERSON. Just take a deep breath and let it go.

That tenant is dead weight anyhow.

As the captain of your ship, it's your job to throw their ass overboard, clean up their mess, and drive on. That's how real leaders take action. They don't curl up and cry. They accept responsibility for whatever has happened. They rub some dirt on their wounds, they drink water, and they keep going. That's how you succeed.

I'm often reminded of the leadership training I had in the Army. I owe most of what I have today to the sound fundamental principles that I absorbed in the field. The thing that rings most true, even today, is the NCO Creed I included in the last chapter.

"No one is more professional than I..."

The creed begins. That may not mean much to you, but to me, it means that at all times, I will hold myself to the highest standard. Never will I let a tenant, contractor, or underpaid spiteful city worker get under my skin. I will always do my best to set the bar high.

This mentality will set a great tone for your relationship with your tenants. Having your tenants always recognize you as a professional means that they will always know you mean business when you come around. I'm not saying don't be friendly. No one wants a jerk for a leader. However, I am saying you probably shouldn't have beers with your tenants. You probably shouldn't invite them to your kid's birthday party, and they shouldn't be calling you if they need something unrelated to your rental. Remain professional with them, and that's how they should treat you back. Doing otherwise is going to make it hard when they're late on rent.

"Competence is my watchword..."

The second paragraph of the NCO creed begins with this line. It means that no matter what, you're going to do something efficiently and successfully. This is always on your mind. Doing your best. Being your best.

Keeping this attitude is going to mean that your properties are always going to get the best repairs you can provide. Your tenants are always going to get the best service they can get, and you're always going to handle your finances with the care that they require.

The reason I'm in business is that I bought buildings

that weren't being cared for. The previous landowners didn't try to take care of their tenants and properties the best they could. They either were absent, didn't care, or intentionally milked the property for what they could. These are weak leaders. These are leaders that don't deserve to have people look to them for guidance.

The next paragraph goes on to say, "My two basic responsibilities will always be uppermost in my mind – accomplishment of my mission and the welfare of my soldiers."

The Army breeds into everyone from the start the idea that leaders take care of those under them and that, regardless of your rank, you complete your mission. Period. There is nothing else. You take care of those under you, and you complete your mission. That basically summarizes everything you learn in the military.

"I know my soldiers and I will always place their needs above my own"

With tenants, it's no different. Your tenants need to be the first and last thing you consider when you make decisions that affect them. Shocker, I know, but your tenants are not money trees that you shake c-notes out of each month. They're living, breathing humans, and landlord-tenant law says you're going to make sure that they have a hospitable place to live.

I could spend most of this book drawing parallels between something as simple as the NCO creed and your responsibilities as a landlord, but I think the point is made.

Great Property Leaders don't bark orders and shake a money tree. They inspire others by remaining professional, staying competent, taking care of those under them, and never taking advantage.

Weak leaders are missing most of what I've highlighted so far. You'll know a weak leader when you see one.

- Weak leaders are not confident.
- They're not decisive.
- They're not in charge.
- They're afraid to be wrong.
- They're afraid to take responsibility for anything.
- They're too risk-averse.
- They don't listen to others.
- They crumble under pressure.
- They dwell on their problems.

Confidence is key in a great leader. **Weak leaders lack confidence.** A lack of confidence is like blood in the water to someone who wants to take advantage. It also stinks to those who want to follow you. Imagine trying to follow a leader into combat who isn't sure about which way to go. You'd look at that person like they were an idiot who was about to get you killed. Tenants are no different. Do you think a tenant is going to respect a landlord who isn't confident enough to enforce standards? I think not.

Being decisive is another key trait that great leaders need. This also falls under confidence. If you can't make a decision, then you're a crap leader. Of course, not every decision you make as a leader is going to be perfect. In fact, I can guarantee that some decisions you make are going to be 100% wrong. You might have bad information.

Someone might be misleading you or scamming you. You may have done everything right and just caught a bad stroke of luck. Honestly, it doesn't matter. Great leaders know that sometimes you make bad choices, and that's okay. What's important is learning from your mistakes, picking yourself up by your bootstraps, and trying again.

Great leaders know that they're wrong sometimes. Once again, and I can't say this enough, it's okay to fail. You're going to make mistakes from time to time. You're going to be wrong. You're going to say and do dumb things sometimes. It happens. We're only human. What really matters is how you handle it when it happens. Weak leaders are going to crumble when the shit goes sideways. They're going to wonder why they've got it so hard. Why they're so unlucky. Why things can't work out for them. The strong leader learns from the mistake and immediately pivots to handle the situation the correct way.

Weak leaders also have a problem with being in charge. Sure, they might bark orders sometimes, but more often than not, they're just not in charge.

If you let your tenants make the calls, then they will. If you ask them if you can raise their rent, do you think they'd allow it? If you ask them if you can come in to do repairs on the weekend, do you think they'd be okay with it? What if you don't enforce a late fee when they decide to pay rent on the 3rd instead of the first? Do you think that they'll respect the rent due date next month?

These are all things that I didn't make up. These are things that real landlords have experienced, I included. Just head over to any industry forum and see for yourself. Almost daily, you'll find new posts from landlords having trouble getting tenants to agree to X, Y, or Z.

Listen here, Property Leaders. You don't get your tenants to agree to anything other than signing the lease. From that point forward, you're the boss of the apple sauce. You need to be in charge. If you're not, your tenants will walk all over you. No question.

Weak leaders are really afraid to take responsibility. I can't tell you how obnoxious this is. I see this a ton in the corporate world, and this is probably my number one reason for wanting to dump all my spare cash into rentals. I really hate leaders who can't own up to mistakes. Nothing is more off-putting than a coward for a leader.

Being afraid to take responsibility is the biggest taboo of leadership in my book. If you're put in charge, then YOU are the only person to blame. If you're working on a project and it isn't done in time, it's your fault. If you finish your project on time, but something isn't right, then it's your fault. If your tenants break something in your house and you let it go, then it's your fault. If you miss your mortgage because your tenants didn't pay rent on time, you guessed it; it's your fault. The bank isn't going to go knock on your tenant's door and ask why they didn't pay rent. They're going to foreclose on you.

You need to take responsibility for everything that happens with your team, the property, everything. This is the only way to fix problems quickly. In fact, it puts you in the driver's seat of the problem-fixing bus.

Tenant intentionally breaks something in the unit out

of spite? Great, tell them they're paying to fix it, or they can find a new place to live.

Contractor doesn't finish the job on time? Awesome, they won't get any more jobs from you in the future.

Rent late? Three-day eviction notice on the following day.

If you jump in the driver's seat, then you can quickly fix problems. Otherwise, you're going to wait for other people to solve your problems, and if you haven't figured it out already, no one gives two craps about you or your problems. Especially your tenants.

Another issue that weak leaders have is that they're too risk-averse. You have to be comfortable taking risks sometimes. Taking a little risk from time to time is important. **Weak leaders are afraid to risk anything**, and they often fail because of it.

Strong leaders know that risk-taking is not only important but that it's key to getting out ahead. I'm not saying to blindly take risks. Great leaders know how to manage and mitigate risk.

One excellent way to manage risk is to always calculate the downside. I don't think I've ever entered a deal where my downside was almost nothing, but the upside was huge. That's just not the way the world works. To deal with this, some of the most successful people in history manage their risk by always knowing the downside of it before they take action. If you always know what your downside is and you're able to accept that downside, then the upside is always going to be icing on the cake when it happens.

Weak leaders like to hide from the downside. They're the ones that won't look at their bank account because they don't want to know how little they have in there. They're afraid to know the truth.

Weak leaders are the ones that are afraid to go inspect a unit after a tenant has left. They're the ones that would rather keep doing the same thing over and over because they're afraid of the risks of growth.

The biggest risk of hiding from the downside is avoiding consulting with experts for things like taxes and home inspections. The weak leader is afraid of what the experts will expose. This is where a lot of people run into trouble. This is often where people take huge hits in the real estate market. All because they were too afraid.

Being able to listen to others is another key trait that weak leaders are missing. Much like being afraid of the downside, they're afraid to get opposing views to their own. They're afraid of new ideas. They're afraid of bad news. They often think that they know everything, that they're smarter than everyone else, so they have nothing to gain from listening.

Strong leaders know that it's important to see every angle they can. They value the mentorship of those above them, and they know that listening to those under them can reveal information that they didn't have before. Strong leaders know that their followers are closest to the front line and have the best knowledge about problems facing the team.

It takes more than just listening to others to be a great leader, though. You can't crumble under pressure when things get tough. When things get tough, weak leaders fold like origami. They quit when things start to heat up. They buckle when they're confronted with complex problems.

Strong leaders look at pressure as a chance to perform. They like to take challenges head-on, and they go at them right up the middle.

Strong leaders relish their opportunities to perform and to prove their metal. This is one of the key differences between the two. Great leaders know that there are always going to be tough times. It's just a matter of how you deal with them.

This brings me to my final bullet on weak leaders. **They dwell on problems.** Weak leaders often dwell on their problems. They tend to have woe-is-me attitudes, and they wait for others to solve problems for them. Worse, some even hide from their problems, hoping they'll go away.

You can't be a little baby about every little thing that pops up. This childish behavior has no room in a successful business. Could you imagine if a company like Walmart was afraid to pay their bills so they "lost" the invoice under a stack of papers? The shareholders would go nuts.

So to summarize this chapter, I'd like to leave you with a story from my time in the service.

Getting 150+ people ready to leave for a combat tour in Iraq can't be an easy task. I was lucky enough to be a low-ranking soldier when we left. My only responsibilities in combat were the people to my left and right. Keep your gun clean, do what you're told, and remember your training. That was the long and the short of it.

Our First Sergeant (the highest-ranking Non-

Commissioned Officer in our company) was a tough guy. As a low-ranking soldier, I should have had as little interaction with him as possible. Most soldiers are afraid of their First Sergeant. This was especially true of ours since he was mean as hell. For good reason, though. It ultimately rested on his shoulders to make sure we were all ready. If we were under-trained in shooting, we'd miss our targets, and we'd lose battles. If we weren't well trained in emergency medical procedures, then people would die. These factors had to have weighed heavily on him.

I was never deterred by any of these things, though. I remember one time shortly before we left for Iraq, they gave a special treat to the top physically fit soldiers from each platoon. They had a couple of training slots open for hand-to-hand combat training with the Special Forces group that was stationed on Fort Lewis with us. I was near the top of our platoon for physical fitness, so I was selected. It was great training and a great honor to learn from SF. These individuals were very nice to us. They're some of the highest trained and most deadly people on the planet, but every single one is more humble than the last.

Well, after one of the training sessions, we were walking back to our barracks when our First Sergeant, who remember is mean as hell, yelled out his office window and asked if we had learned anything.

Being the smart-ass, cocky, looking-to-prove-himself soldier that I was, I said

"I sure did, and if you'd like to see, come on out of your office, and I'll show you."

You better believe that he dropped what he was doing, came outside into the grass, and balled me up like a pretzel in about ten seconds flat. He was super busy. He was a tough leader. Most everyone feared interacting with him. However, he was never afraid to get dirty. He was never afraid to communicate with his soldiers. And most importantly, he was never afraid of a challenge. Especially a challenge from a soldier who was 150 pounds soaking wet.

On a personal note, if you ever read this, First Sergeant Schultz, thanks for being a great example. You and the leadership team you built impacted my life in so many positive ways. These days I often think back on how great of a leader you were, and I wish that you lived closer so I could pull inspiration from you still.

It's people like him who shape our country and even the world. Could you imagine if my old First Sergeant was afraid of conflict or if he weren't confident? Who would follow him? Who would want to listen to him? Who would respect him? It's a tall order for any soldier, and it's also a tall order for your tenants. Don't ask that of them by being a weak leader.

CHAPTER 3

LEADERS EAT LAST

"The servant-leader is servant first. It begins with the natural feeling that one wants to serve, to serve first. Then conscious choice brings one to aspire to lead." — Robert K. Greenleaf

---

I TITLED this chapter "Leaders Eat Last" because this was probably the most profound thing I took from my time in the Army. During my experience in Iraq, I gained a lot of perspective on life. Combat was very eye-opening and spiritual for me. When I say spiritual, I'm referring to a very strong connection with who I am as a person. Combat clarified for me my love for life and how much I hated taking it from others. The experience motivated me to be a better person in life and to give back as much as I can.

When I returned from Iraq, I decided I wasn't going to waste my time left on Earth. All the problems in our country seemed so small to me. Bills, breakups, getting cut off on the freeway. They all seemed so petty when you compared them to war, poverty, and starvation.

Returning from Iraq, I knew right away that I owed it to the friends that I lost to make the most of my life. Nothing seemed impossible to me anymore.

With my solid work ethic and my will to do right by others, I was going to make a change for the better. So, with that in mind, I want to briefly cover the foundation that I believe every great Property Leader needs. These are the concepts that I implement every single day in my property management business.

GREAT PROPERTY LEADERS UNDERSTAND THEIR RELATIONSHIP WITH TENANTS.

One key idea that I took from the military is the symbiotic relationship that exists between leaders and followers. A shitty leader doesn't see this relationship. In fact, they would likely argue that it doesn't exist at all. A great leader would tell you though that if this relationship weren't there, they would be a failure because being a great leader relies so much upon it.

Crap leaders tell you that they issue an order and the follower listens. A great leader knows that the relationship between them and their followers goes much deeper than this.

THEY KNOW THAT IN ORDER TO GET THINGS DONE, THEY NEED TO INSPIRE THEIR FOLLOWERS TO DO THEM.

It's important for your followers to believe in your goals, otherwise, they're not going to want to accomplish them. They will likely just go through the motions of accomplishing the goal to make you happy, spending very little time or effort on it.

You're probably wondering how this all applies to being a landlord, and I'm getting there. All these same leadership lessons apply to your tenants. I'll cover more on how this works in later chapters, but I promise you that if your tenants are inspired to keep things neat, keep the house secure, keep the common areas clean, and not waste water, your life will be much easier. Most importantly though, your people will be taken care of and you'll turn a profit.

THEY KNOW THAT THEIR FOLLOWERS MUST TRUST THEM.

Tenants aren't that much different from soldiers when it comes to following a leader. The soldier must trust their leader. The soldier must know that the leader makes decisions based on their best interest. Soldiers always look to their leaders to set good examples and to be honest. Leaders trust that their soldiers will uphold the military values. These values of trust bind soldiers to their leaders in combat. They're the lynchpin in the leader-follower relationship and without it, they would fail.

Followers need to know a few things.

- They need to know that they can trust you will do what you've said you're going to do.
- They need to trust you won't take advantage of them
- They need to trust that no matter what, you have righteous intentions in your actions.

If any of these pillars of trust are missing, then you're going to have a very hard time inspiring followers to do anything.

If these pieces are there though, you can rest assured that when you tell a tenant to do something that they don't want to do, they're going to know that you're ordering it because it needs to be done, not because you're being mean or don't like them.

One way to build trust is to show that you can listen. Great leaders will always listen in every direction. They know that if you don't listen to what others have to say, you miss important pieces. Showing that you can listen to everyone is a sign of respect. Followers that respect their leaders are easy to inspire to get things done. It's as easy as that.

Something that I remember distinctly from my time in the Army was that those with boots on the ground, know the situation best. This means that the people that are on the front line tend to have the best information.

If you don't live in your rentals, you are detached from the day-to-day minutia. So listen to your tenants. Build a working communication channel with one or two people in each building. This will allow you to get up-to-date situation reports. This is nice if you have contractors you want to keep an eye on, a tenant that is causing problems that must be caught in the act, or even keeping squatters out of vacant units.

I always try to make sure my tenants know they can reach out to me if they see something that doesn't look correct. I'd rather get a hundred reports of things I don't care about than zero reports when the basement has three feet of water in it. If you can't listen to others, then you can't make informed decisions. If you can't make informed decisions, then you can't be an effective leader. It's that simple.

Another important note on listening to others is being able to pivot on decisions you've made. I have a great example of this. When I took over my third four-unit building, I wanted to make sure that the tenants knew I had no plans on shaking things up. The rent was market value and the tenants, for the most part, were fine. This building was in rough shape and needed repairs, but that's the easy part. So, I decided that right after I took the building over, I was going to go and introduce myself to everyone. I wanted to get off on the right foot with them and onboard them into my process as smoothly as possible.

I spent time rehearsing what I was going to say in my head.

"Hello, I'm the new property owner. I want you all to know that I'm going to rehab this building and make all your living conditions much better very soon. No one is getting evicted and no one's rent is changing. Just make sure your rent is in by 5pm. on the first of the month (which is included in their lease) and everything will be great. "

I know that tenants always get worried when a new owner takes over, so I couldn't wait to put them all at ease. I was so excited. I went to the building shortly after getting the keys and I found the first unit. I knocked and was greeted a few minutes later. I smiled and gave my pitch.

Within about 20 seconds of me finishing, the tenant started losing it. She was crying and swearing and said something along the lines of

"You might as well evict me now".

I was taken aback; I had no idea what I'd said wrong. I knew I was an abrasive person, but I thought for sure that my message was about as positive as one could be, next to someone showing up with a giant novelty check for a million dollars.

I asked the tenant what the problem was, and she explained to me that she received a check on the third of the month. This was her monthly income. She always paid rent on the third in the past.

Now, I'm a nice guy, but at the same time, I don't let people pull one over on me. In the past when I've taken over buildings, the tenants tended to push me. Sometimes, tenants act like children. On occasion, they test their boundaries to see what they can get away with. Immediately I assumed this was her game. Try and trick the landlord into letting her pay on the third instead of the first. Here I am trying to be nice and the first tenant I meet thinks I'm a sucker.

So, I told her "Well, your lease is pretty clear. It says

that you pay on the first of the month and the previous owner..."

(who was a shit bag by the way, but more on that later)

"...didn't tell me anyone was on a modified payment schedule. So, you're going to need to figure out a way to make sure you're paying on time."

This, of course, was basically like throwing gasoline on a fire. I realized pretty quickly how stupid I was and that she was telling the truth. This tenant received a form of government subsidy, so it rarely, if ever, came in on the first. This was one of my first experiences with a low-income tenant on government subsidies, but not my last.

So instead of continuing to push back on her, my military leadership skills kicked in. I stopped, removed any emotion that I may have been feeling at the moment, listened to what the tenant was telling me, and thought rationally about the situation.

I told her that paying on the third was fine and that it wouldn't be a problem going forward. When I rewrote her lease, I would correct the rent payment date in it, and she would be good to go. I also made sure to emphasize that I do not mess around with rent. I told her that if she tried to pay on the fourth, she could expect a three-day eviction notice on the 5th. She understood the system, agreed to it and everything was good. She calmed down and everything was fine once again.

So, without much effort on my part, I managed to undo a bad decision just by listening.

Listening to the people under you is imperative if you want to run a successful rental business. I could have easily told her to pound sand and to pay by the first or get out, but this would have no doubt ended in eviction and a loss of rent, immediately after I'd taken this cash-flowing building over. A no-win situation is never the option you want to take. Sure, the rent comes in a couple of days later than I expected, but it's one more unit cash flowing and one less thing to contend with while onboarding a new building. Besides, if there really was a long term issue with accepting rent on the third of the month, then I could easily just tell the tenant that at the end of their lease they would need to find a new place to go and then replace the tenant with someone who better fit what I was looking for in this building. There was no reason to take on this task right at that moment.

THEY TREAT PEOPLE RIGHT.

Nothing, and I mean NOTHING is worth doing in this world if you have to step on others to achieve it. We all stand on the shoulders of giants at some point in our life to get ahead, but that's much different than stepping on people to further your own agenda. There's a distinct difference between using other's knowledge or skills and taking advantage of others because you can. Eventually, bad actions will catch up to you.

If you treat people right, even if you fail, you can sleep well at night. I've certainly failed at things in my rental career. It's going to happen. However, if you don't take advantage of the people that are relying on you, then you'll be able to sleep knowing that even though you failed, you're not a shitty person also.

THEY TAKE CARE OF OTHERS.

You never know what someone is going through. When all your time is consumed with getting carpets cleaned, sinks fixed, bills paid, rent collected, and so on, it's easy to forget that other people have difficulties in life. Help others when you can and when things are tough, you'll still feel good. I've never woken up in the middle of the night and been upset that I stopped to help a stranger change a tire. I've never been mad that I showed kindness to someone when I didn't have to. Doing good things for others will ground you as a leader and help you remember whom you're serving.

Just so we're clear here, as a landlord, YOU are serving the tenants. Not the other way around. Remember that.

GREAT PROPERTY LEADERS AREN'T AFRAID TO GIVE BACK.

No matter who you are, someone helped you at some point to get where you are. So it doesn't matter if it's donating a dollar to your favorite local charity, doing volunteer work for someone, or teaching a free class of something you know, it's important to give back. Giving back will not only make you feel good, but it also feeds the community and helps others grow to have their own success.

Be a mentor at your local school or church. I spent a few years teaching k-12 kids computer science in my free time. The software engineering field is a great field to be in and we certainly need more people. I also taught Girls

Who Code for a little, which is a great program and I'd recommend everyone give it a try.

I did all this work for free because I wanted to give others the opportunities that I had to learn. Another important point to note is that I was broke when I was doing these projects. You don't need to be rich to give back. I often hear from former students that they loved learning computer science, and nothing makes me happier when I do hear from them.

Obviously, you don't need to go learn to code in order to work with kids. There's plenty of other great programs out there. The point isn't what you're teaching, the point is that giving back, especially to the next generation, is one of the most important things you can do. It's usually, if not always, free to do, and it will help keep you grounded. Knowing what's most important in life is the best way to achieve success.

THEY DON'T LET OTHERS WALK ON THEM.

I know this one seems a little out of left field considering most of what I have said up to this point has been about giving back and taking care of others.

You can be a caring person that doesn't take crap from anyone though. When you start to show that you are a giving person, people will try and take advantage of that. This doesn't mean you shouldn't stand up for yourself. Great leaders know that they walk quietly but carry a big stick. Don't be afraid to smack someone with it if they cross the line. Metaphorically, of course.

If you let people walk on you, you're going to have a

hard time being a landlord. Contractors and tenants will take advantage of you and you'll lose money and opportunities along the way. If someone is trying to overcharge you, tell them you don't think the price is fair. If a tenant tells you you'll get your rent when they feel like it, then evict them. Stand up for yourself or you'll be the next failed landlord who gave their tenant six months of free housing because they were too much of a coward to stand up to them and demand rent.

THEY DON'T LET NEGATIVE COMMENTS TEAR THEM DOWN.

Finally, don't let negative comments tear you down. If I had a dollar for every time someone said something negative to me about myself or my business, I'd be sitting on a beach right now getting fanned with a palm tree leaf.

People love to tear others down. It's almost like a sport it seems. My favorites are the people that tell me that I can't do something for X, Y, and Z reasons, that I'm already doing. Don't fall victim to comments like this. These people are usually cowards who are too afraid to make changes in their own lives. They try to tear you down to their level so they don't have to come up to yours. It's much easier to tear others down than it is to pull others up, and most people take the easy path. Don't be like most people. You'll find that by constantly helping and motivating others to come up to your level, you're going to grow much faster.

Just remember to kill 'em with kindness. If someone starts saying hateful things about you or your business, say something nice to them. Tell them how happy you are and how great it feels to help others. Either they'll get the message, or they'll go hide under whatever bridge they usually troll from.

I don't let people put barriers of negativity in front of me. I look them square in the eye and tell them not only why I can do something, but also how I'm going to do it. I say it with so much confidence that it doesn't matter how negative they're being. My positivity crushes them like the disgusting bugs they are. Then I move on with life and forget that person exists because my energy is much better used elsewhere.

So, you're probably asking yourself at this point, "Why do leaders eat last?"

Simply put, it's because the people under you come first.

It doesn't matter if it's a soldier about to charge into combat or a low-income tenant in a bad part of town. If they follow you, you make sure they're taken care of first. That's your job. You put their priorities first and you eat last.

Do this and the money will follow.

CHAPTER 4

CAPTAIN OF THE SHIP

"The pessimist complains about the wind. The optimist expects it to change. The leader adjusts the sails." — John Maxwell

---

THE CAPTAIN.

They're confident.

They're decisive.

They're always calmly in charge.

Is this you? Odds are that if you picked up this book, it probably isn't. That's okay, though. Continue to read this book. Let its lessons sink in. The fact that you're trying to grow as a leader means you're on your way. You just need to find your voice.

Why is it important for a Property Leader to embody the four qualities listed above?

Simple. People don't respond to or want to comply

with indecisive cowards. They might believe that they want someone soft and easygoing, but in all reality, most people are just looking to follow someone willing to make difficult decisions and provide a sense of direction.

Think about a time in your life that you were part of a great team. What would have happened on that team if your team leader were unable to make a decision, or if they faltered or second-guessed themself under pressure? In all likelihood, the answer is anarchy until someone else stepped into the leadership role and made a strong choice.

Leaders who can't decide are only leaders in the title, and they get walked on. Their troops think they're a joke and undermine them. Their subordinates override the leader's decisions, and, most importantly, when it's crunch time, chaos ensues.

Tenants are no different. Fear and indecisiveness in a leader stink, and they can smell it. It's like blood in the water. So what are you supposed to do? Everyone is afraid at some point in life. I constantly make decisions that scare the hell out of me. Everything from buying buildings in new, lower-income areas to deciding to evict someone in court scares me. Being afraid is normal and natural, and if you can manage your fear, it can be a great tool.

I use fear to help me make sure my bases are covered. When I start looking at new buildings to buy, I use fear to guide me in mitigating risk. I mitigate risk by making sure I play out every possible scenario in my mind.

What happens if the rent is $100 lower per unit per month than I expected? What happens if the building has an unknown issue that needs resolving upon purchase? What happens if ....

Over and over and over I ask myself these questions. I use fear as my guide to the questions, and I use rationalism to come up with answers that mitigate my risk. For example:

What happens if the rent is $100 lower per unit per month than I expected?

I should account for this by requiring that I only pay X dollars per unit. This way, if I've overestimated the rent, I can still afford the mortgage. If they don't budge on the price, then I can mitigate it by having cash in reserves and possibly upgrading the units so that they are valued where I need them to be.

Fear should help you ask questions, and your rational brain should help you answer them. Once they're answered, move on. Don't dwell on your fears. That's how fear becomes a problem.

Fear doesn't just affect your decision-making; it also has a direct correlation to your ability to rent units. "Desperate Renting," as I like to call it, is incredibly toxic to your business. Desperate renting is when you're extraordinarily anxious to rent a unit because if you don't, you're going to start taking large losses. Think about a sleazy car salesperson. Is that the image you want when you're leasing a unit? I sure as heck don't, but I've been there. In fact, I've been there A LOT. I'm a great leader, but I'm a horrible salesperson. I have no filters, I'm usually overly honest, and I have lost countless potential tenants with my big mouth. I learned my lesson eventually, and you will too if you suffer from this.

Imagine you have a tenant that decided to leave for

whatever reason. You, in turn, fix up the property and list it. Two days go by.

Six days go by.

Two weeks go by.

No one responds to your ad.

You only have 30 more days of rent flowing in before you have to pay out of pocket, and you start getting worried. This is the Desperate Renting Danger Zone.

In the Desperate Renting Danger Zone, the stakes are high. You're likely to scare off good tenants, and the ones you don't scare off, you probably don't want anyway. Those people are more desperate to find a place than you are to lease it. People who are super desperate to find an apartment very likely have reasons why. Maybe they have bad credit, they were just evicted, or they're deep in debt. The list goes on. Regardless, it's not a situation you want to put yourself in.

So how do you overcome desperation? Well, first, you need to realize that you, and you alone, control the way you feel. If I can borrow the words of Tony Robbins, you are in charge. You can choose to feel any way you want. Right now, imagine the happiest day of your life and put yourself there. Imagine the way it made you warm inside, the smile you had on your face, the good feelings that rushed through you. You could probably do that, and you probably can feel some of that positivity even right now, just by changing your focus for a few moments. You are in control of the way you feel, so don't let discouraging thoughts about your property scare you into feeling desperate to rent it. Your feelings about the property will come across in your showing, so make sure they're positive ones.

Prior to the day you plan on showing the unit, you need to ask yourself the following questions.

What makes the apartment great?

What makes this area desirable?

What did you see in this property when you bought it?

Are you across from a school? Near a park?

What is the city doing to improve the area?

What do you offer that other landlords don't?

You need to run through this list prior to showing your unit and build up your confidence. If you can be confident about how great your product is, then the people that are on the fence about renting will be happy to put in an application.

Personally, I've always struggled with the sales aspect of the landlording cycle. I'm just not a natural salesperson. One resource that helped me improve greatly is *The Way Of The Wolf: Straight Line Selling* by Jordan Belfort. This book highlights a very clear sales pipeline for you to work from. It hasn't made me the perfect salesperson, but it has absolutely improved my leasing process immensely and increased my confidence in selling tenfold. I recommend it to anyone struggling with that aspect of their business.

Remember, desperation stinks, and when you're desperate to rent, you'll make bad choices. The captain is never desperate. The captain of the ship is always calm, cool, and collected, even under pressure. You don't always get to choose when you're going to have to face challenges. Often, challenges will catch you by surprise. You need to always keep a cool mind to make good choices. Just take a breath, think, and most importantly, take action.

I often think about the saying "never let them see you bleed" when I think about losing self-control in front of a tenant. Most tenants will just respect you less if you bleed in front of them. The conniving tenants, and you will have them, will attempt to use it to their advantage. Keep your problems between you and the people that aren't going to leverage them against you.

I want to share another personal experience with you. A few years before writing this book, I had a tenant in a solid B neighborhood who was moving out. This tenant had never really been too much of an issue. She had a problem with a neighbor once, but it was resolved, and life went on as it typically does.

For the most part, this was a typical tenant. She was a young, college-age professional who paid on time, kept to herself, and never really reported anything to me. Honestly, in the three or so years she lived there, I don't think I had any maintenance issues from her. I tend to keep my properties in pretty good working order, so that's not super uncommon. As soon as repairs come in, no matter how big or small, I try to get them done. Right now, we have a 72-hour turnaround (or less) for almost all issues.

So this tenant was moving out and I was tasked with flipping her unit. All of my tenants know from day one that I have an established move-out process. They give me 60 days' notice before leaving. In those 60 days, I inspect the unit for mandatory repairs, I complete the repairs, and the unit is listed, shown, and rented. All of this happens before the tenant ever moves out. This is one aspect of how I keep an extraordinarily low vacancy rate.

So, I started the process, and there wasn't anything major to deal with. I noticed that there were some paint touch-ups to be done, but for the most part, the unit just needed a steam cleaning, and then it would be ready for the next tenant. That is assuming the tenant didn't do any major damage on move out or leave the place trashed. That's pretty uncommon in this building, so I don't usually expect that, but I do account for it just in case.

Everything had gone as expected. The repairs were done, and the new tenant was leased and waiting to move in. All I needed to do was collect the keys, do a quick walkthrough to make sure the unit was empty, and get the steam cleaner in there. Then the next day, I would do a final walkthrough, and the new tenant would get the keys and move in.

I met up with the exiting tenant on move-out day. She and her partner waited outside for me while I went up to inspect the empty unit. As soon as I walked in, I noticed something wrong. There was a giant, and I do mean GIANT, solid wax puddle on the floor in the middle of the dining room. Now, thankfully this wax was almost the same color as the carpet (cream), so I didn't expect a major stain. I also figured the steam cleaner could get it out. This guy that I hire has always worked miracles for me. It's important that when you find good contractors, you hang onto them, as I'll discuss in a later chapter.

So, I went back outside to get the keys. The tenant was standing and waiting, with her partner standing awkwardly behind her on her phone.

Immediately, the tenant said,

"So, we're good to go?"

"Yup, I'll do a final inspection tomorrow," I said, knowing that I wanted to wait and see if that stain came out before I gave a definitive answer.

Then she asked,

"So, I get my full deposit back?"

It was at this point that I knew she was worried about the stain, so I decided to address it as bluntly as possible.

"Well, I need to make sure that the carpet cleaner can get that giant puddle of wax out of the floor. If it doesn't come out, you're going to be liable for it."

The tenant went into a rage and started throwing everything she had at me.

"That stain was there when I moved in!" she insisted.

"No, it wasn't, and I have photos of the unit prior to you moving in that will verify that. Also, prior to every tenant moving in, I have the apartment professionally steam cleaned, after which, I do a full walkthrough and inspect the results" I said.

"Well, it wasn't there the second I moved in, but a few days later, it appeared. You're going to give me my full deposit back." She demanded.

I could see this was only going to get uglier from there, and we were in front of my building and within earshot of existing tenants. Even though I wanted to tell this woman how much of a liar she was and how if she didn't like this, she could take me to court, I instead remained cool, calm, and collected.

"How about this," I started. "The state allows me 30 days to return your deposit. How about I have the carpet steam cleaned, and I inspect it in a couple of weeks. If the stain returns, you won't be charged anything for it. If not, though, you'll be responsible for the cost of the steam clean at least."

The tenant could tell that this was a reasonable option with which she couldn't argue, so she instead said, "Fine, whatever," and left.

The carpet was steam cleaned, and, as you might have already guessed, the wax came out and the stain never returned. Since no permanent damage was done, I returned the tenant's deposit and charged her only for the $80 steam clean. After that, I never heard from her again.

It wasn't until after they walked away that I realized an important piece to all this, which made me very glad I'd remained calm and rational. The tenant's partner, standing awkwardly behind the tenant and on her phone as the tenant spoke with me, was recording the exchange. They were planning to get me on video saying that she would get her full deposit back so that if I charged her for the stain, they could take me to court.

This was something that I had never considered happening, but it did. Boy, was I happy I stayed calm. It put a damper on their little plan to entrap me and everything worked out in my favor.

The key takeaways from this story are as follows:

- **I stuck to my script.** I had a plan going in, and I made sure that no matter what happened, I followed my plan. First, I do a quick walkthrough to make sure the unit is empty. Then I collect the keys, and after I physically have control of the property, I do a final walkthrough.

- **I called upon my standard operating procedures.** Because of my standard operating procedures, I was able to confidently say that I knew the stain hadn't been on the carpet when the tenant moved in. Having SOPs takes the pressure off of you when things go sideways.

- **I remained cool, calm, and collected.** I was professional at all times while dealing with the tenant. The only thing they got on camera was how courteous and reasonable I was. I bet that'd look pretty good for me in court.

- **Their attempt to lock me into saying something wrong was foiled** and I was able to recover the money for the cleaning out of the tenant's deposit. Know the laws. Know what you can and can't do. It makes fighting battles like this a cakewalk.

CHAPTER 5

COMMAND RESPECT

"I believe the first test of a truly great man is in his humility." — *John Ruskin*

BEFORE I GOT SERIOUSLY into real estate investing, I was just getting by. I lived in this crappy little one-bedroom apartment with my three-year-old son. It was in an extremely low-income area and I certainly belonged there at the time. I was using my GI Bill to get my degree in software engineering. The GI bill has a small living allowance, so I was able to survive while going to school full time, but it wasn't glamorous by any means. I remember saving a dollar or two from my meager lunch budget every day and using it at the end of the week to take my son to Chuck-E-Cheese as a treat. I really knew how to stretch a dollar.

This apartment that we lived in was a shit hole to be

polite. Though I'll always treasure the memories of one-on-one time spent with my son, our experience there was tainted by the poor leadership of those running the place.

The property management company that managed this building was run by idiots and the repairs were slow if they ever happened at all. I distinctly remember one spring when our ceiling caved in from water sitting on the roof. Two months went by before they sent anyone over to even look at it. I eventually had to withhold the rent to get them to do anything to help us. These scumbags had no problem taking my rent each month, but they couldn't be bothered to send someone over to fix the water pouring in through the ceiling in our bedroom. Their advice was to sleep in the living room until it was fixed.

I knew there and then that if I were ever able to start buying rentals, I would never treat people that way. Tenants are not money trees. I can't say this enough. If you're in charge of taking care of a building, then that means you're in charge of making sure the people inside that building are living in hospitable conditions. If you can't provide hospitable conditions for your tenants, then they'll never respect you. Even back then, with almost no property management experience, I didn't respect that management company. Today, I know the struggles of running a successful property management company and I respect that company even less now.

Why?

I respect them less now than ever because I know that it's not hard to schedule a repair person to fix something in a reasonable amount of time. I know that if you're running your books correctly, there's plenty of margin for repairs. I respect them less now because it's clear to me that it was blatant disrespect that made them so inefficient. They wanted the respect from the tenants. They demanded we pay our rent on time, but they couldn't reciprocate that respect. That's a problem. It's a clear sign of poor leadership and I swore that it'd never happen when I started managing my properties. That company better hope I'm never in a position to buy it out because if I did, the first thing I'd do is clean house.

Commanding respect can be a tough thing for some people and it's a hard concept to explain. I can tell you what it's not though. It's not ordering someone to do something. It's not demanding that something be done a certain way. It's not one-way communication.

You'll know leaders who command respect because when other people talk about them, they'll say things like

"They're a hard ass, but I totally get what they're saying".

They're the ones that when they walk into the room, they don't have to say a word and the people under them yield conversation to hear what they have to say. Leaders who command respect are able to easily inspire others to do things in order to achieve a common goal.

Many don't want to hear this, but leaders who command respect often aren't the most well-liked people. There were plenty of leaders I've had in the past that I hated to my bones. Yet, I would 100% follow them to the depths of hell if I had to. That's the funny thing about those types of leaders. They can be the biggest jerks ever, but when they speak, you can't really dispute anything they say. They say and do things that, though they might make them unpopular, need to be said or done to move forward.

When I think about how I can command respect amongst my tenants I always come back to the idea that the best approach is to be fair, professional, and rational at all times. No matter how heated a situation gets, remain fair, professional and rational. If you show tenants that when their world is crumbling, you have the ability to remain calm, you'll earn their respect.

Some tenants are just walking bags of drama. You can't always weed these people out and honestly, everyone needs a place to live. I have tenants that are bags of drama, but they pay their rent on time and they're not really an issue otherwise. We're all human. We're all just in different spots in life. I try not to let a tenant meltdown affect me.

Army leaders don't kowtow to confrontation. In fact, this is something that's drilled into every soldier from day one. You don't shy away from confrontation. You drive right into it, kick it in its face, and take control. You can't be afraid to face your issues head on. Hiding from problems and or confrontations doesn't solve anything. Great leaders will not only tackle their problems head on but they'll try and turn them into an advantage or success.

So how do you tackle problems head on? You simply need to be the alpha. Not every leader has the alpha bone, I understand this., but, everyone can fake it. It's okay to not live and breathe the alpha mentality day in and day out. However, you need to be able to switch into this mode when you're presented with a confrontation or when you need to solve an issue. Remember, people want to follow leaders. They don't want to follow indecisive cowards. Be the alpha. If you can get your tenants into the mindset that you're in charge by leading them with respect and empathy, then they're going to listen more and they're more likely to do what you say. You want your tenants working with you, not against you.

There are plenty of "leaders" out there, and I use that term loosely in this case, who think they should demand respect. But it just doesn't work. No one wants to follow an asshole. People don't like being ordered around. Believe it or not, even people who follow others want respect. Real leaders can inspire others to do what they want. Real leaders have a healthy dose of humility.

So, what are the keys to commanding respect?

- Be honest
- Do what you say you'll do
- Show others that you deserve their respect through your actions

That's basically all you need to gain your tenants' trust. If your tenants know that you're not lying to them, if they know that you'll do what you say you're going to do and they see you respecting others through your actions, then you'll command their respect.

Being honest at all times with your tenants is important. Don't lie to tenants. Even if it's bad news or hard news, there are a lot of dividends to be gained by just being an honest source of information. No matter how much tenants don't like what you tell them, they'll be far angrier if you hide it and it comes to light later. Delivering bad news comes with the job. It sucks, I know. Don't sugar coat things though. Just be honest and deliver the news. Even if your tenants hate you for what you're saying, they'll respect the fact that you told them the truth.

There's another dimension to this as well. Everyone has cell phones these days, and almost all cell phones are able to record audio and video. If you lie to a tenant and they're able to get it on camera, it could destroy you in court. The last thing you want in front of a judge or magistrate is a video of you blatantly lying. Just be honest and remember, no matter what message you have to deliver, it's never personal.

Follow through with what you say you're going to do. If you tell a tenant that you're going to get X,Y or Z cleaned up, then do it. If you tell them that they can expect to get a repair done on a certain day, then make sure it gets done in that time frame. If you can't get it done, give them a call in advance. Days in advance if you can. My tenants know that if I say I'll get something fixed by a certain time, it happens. It doesn't matter if I hire someone to do it or if I have to climb a snow covered mountain with tools strapped to my back and spare keys clenched in my teeth, it gets done.

Tenants who can't trust you will be hard to predict. They might not tell you when things are broken or they may just up and vanish one day. I like to show my tenants that I'm 100% honest with them and this often means that I get 90% honesty back.

Important as it is, gaining the trust of your tenants is only half the battle. There's another major factor in commanding respect.

. . .

Remain Professional

Always remember to remain professional at all times. You never know when something you say may come back to bite you. As I've already discussed, everyone has a camera phone these days. Bet on the fact that tenants will be looking for some sort of leverage against you if they feel threatened. Not only that, but it's difficult to respect someone who lashes out or crumples when difficulty arises, so maintaining your professionalism will make a huge difference there as well. How can you be sure to do this though?

1. Look Presentable

I'm not saying you need to put on a suit and tie every time you visit one of your properties. However, if you live on site and walk around in pajama pants and grubby t-shirts, you won't exactly come across as a professional to your tenants. If you're doing repairs yourself, work clothes are fine, but if you're meeting potential tenants or simply checking in, put some effort into your appearance so they can see that you respect yourself. That makes it much easier for them to then respect you, too.

2. Follow Through

Following through on the promises you make not only builds trust in your tenants, but also supports their perception of you as a professional. This comes down to you treating your property management as a job, not just a hobby or side hustle. When you do that, you're much more likely to prioritize the tasks you must complete for various units or tenants. You'll be sure that repairs are addressed promptly and efficiently and that any promises you make to your tenants are kept. Your tenants will see that you take your property seriously and they will too.

3. **Communicate Respectfully**

Now, coming from the military, this next one is tough for me. Try not to swear if you can help it. Keep things professional. Don't swear, don't lie, don't be hateful, and don't be vindictive. I know it seems silly to have to say these things, but I guarantee you there's some landlord right now reading this and saying to themselves "Oh maybe I shouldn't have retaliated against the tenant for telling me I'm fat and dumb for asking them to close the front door to the building."

Keeping all communications between you and your tenants calm and rational keeps your tenants from thinking of you as emotional or dramatic. This lends you quite a bit of credibility as a respectful communicator and problem solver.

4. **Set Boundaries**

It's great to have tenants you like, and who like you back. In fact, it makes both parties' lives a lot easier. But there is a very fine line to walk between a professional relationship and a casual friendship. To maintain your footing on this line, you should set boundaries between yourself and your tenants. Do check in with them about the unit they are renting. Do not, however, meet up with them for beers on the weekend. Keeping this relationship firmly situated as one of tenant and landlord ensures that they won't panic and hide any accidental damage to a unit, but they also won't try to get away with paying rent late.

This idea of professional relationships also extends to contractors you hire. It's essential to have solid working relationships with any plumbers, electricians, or landscapers you work with. You want to know that they can be relied upon to get the job done in a timely manner and trusted to charge you fairly for the work. This will save you countless headaches and a considerable amount of money. When you find people you like, hold on to them. To ensure that good workers continue to work with you, you'll want to make it worthwhile for them, with respectful interactions, a clear understanding of acceptable contact hours, reasonable turnaround times, and fair rates. But just as with your tenants, you should refrain from getting too comfortable with these contractors. Keep all exchanges professional and you'll keep from falling into awkward situations where people attempt to take advantage of you.

Commanding respect can be tough. Sometimes it takes years to build respect with new tenants, especially if the previous owner was a real tool bag.

Here's an incident that I had with a tenant that highlights the importance of commanding respect.

I had just finished purchasing my second house hack. The rent for the building was about half of what market value was at the time. The new tenants were a ragtag bunch. I probably wouldn't have leased to some of them if they had gone through my vetting process. When you take over a new building, the tenants will sometimes test you and push their boundaries to see what they can get away with. It's important that when you see this, you identify it quickly and you stomp its guts out before it grows out of your control.

It was time to collect the first month's rent from my new tenants. Now before you can expect something from a tenant, you need to make sure that your expectations are clearly laid out in a notice that you send them. Make sure it's written and that they have plenty of time to read it. I issued such a notice when I took the building over. I made it clear to all the tenants that their rent was due by 5pm on the 1st, no exceptions.

At this point in time, I was still doing this by going door to door. I didn't mind though, I liked getting to know my tenants. Two of the three tenants paid their rent on time as outlined in the notice I had delivered. The third tenant, however, chose not to pay on time. They chose to push my time table and see if they could get away with it. Well unfortunately for them, I was ready for this. After the 5pm deadline came and went, I went up to my computer and printed a three day eviction notice. At 8am on the second, I went down to the front door of the tenant that refused to pay on time and in a grandiose manner attached, with bright red tape, a three day eviction notice to their door. I got the rent almost immediately after that.

I had sent a clear message to this tenant and the rest of the tenants that I wasn't fooling around. It also sent a message to the tenant not to test me.

The problem with this approach though is that it's heavy handed. It sets a clear idea in their head what the expectations are, but it also sacrifices any humility that they may have seen in you. When things like this happen, you become less of the guy that bought the building and more of the evil landlord. It's important that after an incident like this, you focus on different ways to rebuild their respect for you. This is where the bullets I listed above come into play. Be honest, do what you say you will, command respect through actions.

When I had first taken this building over, it was a property in distress. The owner prior to me had a horrible contractor that did poor work and likely overcharged him to do it. The repairs were subpar and broke frequently. The tenants even had mice running through their units. It was a bad situation.

On top of all that, the rent was only about 30% of what it could actually be based on the area. It always makes me laugh when I see landlords fail because they didn't set the rent high enough. I'm not sure what's going through their minds at the time. Especially today, when it's so easy to hop online and see what other people are asking for comparable units right next door. When I evaluate a property to buy, 99% of the time I'm sitting in my underwear looking at Craigslist and Zillow. If I can do it, anyone can.

When you walk into a building like this, know that it's going to take time to build respect with the tenants. You have to realize that up until you've taken over, they didn't really have any structure in their building. They thought it was okay to pay whenever they felt like it. They don't know how to listen to the landlord because they've never had one worth listening to. Keep this in mind when you take over a new building, especially one that was in distress.

CHAPTER 6

DELIBERATE & DECISIVE

"Heavy is the head that wears the crown" — *King Henry IV*

WE'RE GOING to start this chapter out with a couple stories and then abstract some lessons out of them. These two stories are, just like all the stories in this book, 100% real events that I've experienced as a property manager. I hope that you're able to learn from my mistakes and gain from my experience.

We'll start the first story with Drunk Rob. Drunk Rob was one of my first tenants. Looking back on this situation now, I could handle it without question, but unfortunately there's no playbook for being a property manager. You learn from your experiences and it's a long path to consistent success with tenants.

Rob was an interesting character. He and his

girlfriend, both easily old enough to be my parents, lived in one of my four family buildings. When I took the building over, it, like all the buildings I acquire, was in rough shape. The building needed work, the rents were well below market value, and the tenants wouldn't usually be my first choice.

After I took this building over, I started the slow process of getting it up and running. Though today, I usually can onboard tenants in a week and fully repair a building in a matter of a couple of months, back then, it took me years to onboard a building. When you're breaking even each month, you're afraid to raise rent, trying desperately to just cover the mortgage and working long nights to fix things yourself. It can be incredibly difficult to maintain what you have, so the last thing you want is turnover.

For about a year after I took the building over, Rob and his girlfriend were fine. They maintained their little garden, they were generally quiet, and they didn't really cause any issues. I did, however, notice that Rob had a drinking problem.

As time went on, the building was repaired, and I needed to start raising rent. I started with Rob and his girlfriend because their rent was the lowest. They were paying $400 a month in an area that could easily fetch $600. That's a big difference when you're breaking even on a building. So, I called the tenants over to my apartment (I lived next to them in the same building) and I started to break the news to them.

Gosh, if I could go back, I'd shake myself by the shoulders and say

"BE DECISIVE, BE DELIBERATE, HAVE CONFIDENCE!"

Lessons learned in blood though are not soon forgotten. I finally came out with it and told them that I was raising their rent. The girlfriend was fine. She had no issue with the rent increase and was happy to resign the new lease. Rob was clearly taking issue with it though. He didn't really say much, but you could tell he had an attitude problem.

A few days passed, and that's when shit really hit the fan. I had just gotten home from work. It was about 5pm in the middle of the week. I had just walked in the front door when I heard a door slam in the back of the house. Now if you've ever lived with other people, you know that this happens from time to time. I've become so accustomed to tenants slamming doors and yelling that I tend to just tune it out.

Then, it happened again, and again. I started hearing yelling. Someone was yelling racial slurs in our back hallway.

Now if you knew me, you'd know that I'm not one to take shenanigans lightly. As a former Army sergeant and a combat proven Military Police Officer, I don't tolerate people slamming my things around and stepping out of line. I absolutely wouldn't tolerate racial bigotry in my building. So naturally, I went to investigate.

As I entered the back hallway, I found Rob, drunk and yelling. He was opening his back door, yelling slurs at me and then slamming it shut. He was apparently upset that I had bought the building and that I had raised his rent. You're going to see this. I've actually experienced it three times now. Long term tenants have a sense of ownership over their units. They feel entitled to them and they don't like someone new stepping in to tell them how things are going to go.

But this was the first time that I had experienced something like this, so I had to think about how to handle it. The Army sergeant in me wanted to stomp his guts out while simultaneously asking him rhetorical questions like "Who do you think you are?" and "Have you lost your mind?"

However, my rational side prevailed.

In a clear and no-nonsense tone, I told Rob that if he didn't stop attempting to break his back door off the hinges, I was going to contact the police and tell them that he's destroying my property. Then, I was going to evict him.

As you might imagine, Drunk Rob has some choice words for me. So, I followed through on my first threat. I immediately contacted the police and informed them that I had a drunk and belligerent tenant yelling racial slurs and attempting to destroy his back door. The police responded and put Rob in his place. They informed him if they were called back again that night that he'd be going to jail for disorderly conduct and destruction of property.

When Rob's girlfriend arrived home, I pulled her aside and explained the situation to her. She was surprisingly understanding. Apparently, Rob's drinking had reached an unsustainable point. I knew I had to do something. It was clear to me that the tenant was conflicted about what to do.

Since the only person on the lease was actually the girlfriend, I told the tenant that she had two choices. She could ride out the remainder of her existing lease and they could both find a new place to go, or, Rob could move out and she could lease the apartment by herself under the condition that he wasn't allowed to stay there as a tenant anymore.

The girlfriend agreed and Rob was removed from the apartment a few days later. The reason I keep referring to her as "the girlfriend" is because it's been eight years now and this woman is still a tenant of mine. She's a very good tenant, she pays on time, she takes care of the property, and she tells me when shenanigans arise. Drunk Rob was never heard from again and she often tells me how nice and peaceful things are over there.

The second story that I want to share with you is a little harder to swallow. It too involves a property that I bought that had existing tenants. The tenants were two senior citizens with an autistic adult child.

When I bought my thirteenth and fourteenth units, a little duplex in a nice area of a C class and D class town, I generally knew what to expect. There would be some carpeting to replace and new appliances to install, some painting to do, and some clean up to take care of. Nothing major. I had walked through this building a couple times and didn't notice anything crazy. I also had a building inspection done that didn't turn up anything major. For the most part, it was a standard, buy, onboard, rehab, and rent situation.

As mentioned in previous chapters, I have pretty strict procedures. One of which is that after buying a building, I do an in-depth walkthrough of each unit to create a repair schedule. I categorize things as "need done,""should be done," "would be nice to have done," and "can be put off but will need done eventually. "

This building was only half occupied, so I started with the side that had tenants in it. I wanted to make sure that they were happy and being taken care of before I started working on the vacant unit.

As I went into the unit, the tenants reassured me how happy they were. They told me all about how they loved the area they were in, how they were long term tenants and that they were afraid I was going to evict them. I assured them that their rent was market value, I had no reason to evict them. Then I started walking through the unit...

The unit was well kept. As I mentioned, I had been through it a few times and each time it appeared clean, organized and hygienic. Until I went into the kitchen.

Now, before I share this next bit, remember the previous property owner from a couple chapters ago? The one who I called a scumbag and promised to elaborate on later? I bought this building from him. All of the terrors I'm about to describe were his doing.

Part of my in-depth walk through is to check all plumbing. I went into the kitchen and started looking at the sink, drains, and faucet. Next, I moved on to the cabinets to make sure there were no loose hinges. Things like that are two-second repairs and tend to prevent damage to the hinges and doors over the long run, so I always check them.

When I opened the cabinet though, I didn't find loose hinges. The hinges worked fine. What I found were roaches running for their lives. Big roaches. The kind of roaches that I have nightmares about on a regular basis now.

These tenants had a kitchen full of roaches. It was possibly the worst case I've ever seen. When I inquired, they said that the previous owner had specifically said not to mention the roaches when I was looking at the property. They told me that the roaches had been there for years. I called the exterminator right away.

The exterminator gave me his report. They told me that the roaches were going to be hard to kill because they were so entrenched in the pantry. The tenants were going to have to remove all of the food from the kitchen, seal it in bins, and keep it there until the roaches were gone, which would probably take weeks. The exterminator had also found bed bugs in their mattresses. Bed bugs, if you don't know, are notoriously hard to get rid of. Doing so requires laundering every piece of linen you have, bagging it, bagging your mattresses, and cleaning everything else you own with alcohol. It's a nightmare for anyone, but especially for two seniors.

I was left with an ethical dilemma. Do I attempt to treat the infestation while the tenants are in place, or do I remove these tenants from their home and start fresh? On one hand, the tenants are living in an inhabitable environment, one which I was now legally required to make habitable for them. So, by removing them, I'm forcing them to move to a place that is hopefully healthier than what they're currently living in. On the other hand, if I kicked them out it was unlikely that they were going to have an easy time finding something. To add to the complexity of the situation, these are extraordinarily low-income tenants. They live off SSI and supplement their income by collecting scrap metal out of the trash (where the bugs likely came from).

It became painfully obvious to me what needed to happen. I was going to have to remove these tenants before I could truly treat the building. It wasn't going to be fun. It wasn't going to be smooth. It was, however, the right thing to do.

These tenants were on a month-to-month lease, so ending their lease legally was pretty easy. I just didn't have to renew it. The state of Ohio only requires that I give them 30 days' notice, but I gave them two months. I also told them they wouldn't need to pay rent for the remainder of their time at the property, in order to help them save for the next place.

That all said, I can't help but feel there's a special place in hell for people that kick out senior citizens with autistic kids.

Once the tenants were informed, they had a breakdown, as expected. They begged and pleaded and attempted to convince me of ways to make it work. I knew though, that the only way for everyone to win was for them to go. The fact of the matter was that there was no way that the infestation was going to be eradicated while these tenants remained in the property. There was no way that I could in good faith lease the other side of the building with this infestation in place. Most importantly though, I couldn't, with a clear conscience, continue to lease an apartment to three people that were depending on me to maintain a safe and healthy environment, knowing that they were living with roaches and bed bugs. Though they

asked me and begged me over the course of a couple weeks,
I stuck to my guns. They had to go.

So, what did we learn from these two examples? We
learned that it's important to be able to make decisions
when things go off the rails. Even if the decision isn't the
optimal one, leaders need to be deliberate and decisive.

In the first example, I clearly told Drunk Rob to stop
what he was doing or there would be consequences. I then
followed through with what I said I was going to do. It
ultimately led to Rob being removed from the property. It
was the loss of a tenant, but his girlfriend remained, and
she's been a great tenant ever since. In fact, to this day she
is my longest leased tenant.

In the second example, we saw a good deal go bad
really quick. Caught in the middle were three of the most
vulnerable tenants you can have. They obviously had a
bias and wanted to remain in the bedbug- and roach-
infested apartment. It was my job as a leader to make a
decision, be deliberate, and be decisive. This decision
wasn't easy. It affected their lives and displaced them. I
knew that their autistic child wouldn't be able to walk to
the library he loved anymore, and I knew that it would be
difficult and stressful for these two seniors to move. I also
knew that it was the only path that led to an outcome
where they weren't in this situation anymore.

When you make a decision, you need to stick with it. If
you have thought out all the different moves, and you have
reached a solution, don't veer off course. Leaders who
make decisions and then go back on those decisions are
viewed as indecisive and weak, and ultimately it will lead
to more problems down the road. Once you reverse a

decision, the tenant knows that there's a chance you'll do it again next time. So, the next hard choice you must make will almost certainly be met with resistance.

Don't be afraid to cut your losses either. It's not easy being king and you're not perfect. Not every decision will be easy, but as long as you keep the best interest of the business and your tenants in mind, you'll be okay. You'll almost always gain more from a tricky situation by recognizing it for what it is and moving forward than by continuing to deliberate.

Decisions aren't always going to be cut and dry. Sometimes, when you're trying to problem solve, you have to make it up as you go. Guess what? There's no road map to solving every problem. That's life. Just remember that any choice is better than no choice at all.

Below are a few action steps to help you cultivate a deliberate and decisive approach to landlording.

Prepare yourself for tears.

You can't buckle when they start crying. Have you ever had a tenant cry? I've had it more times than I'd like to count but it's the reality of this business. Crying is most often a tactic and usually not genuine. Don't let emotions sway you off course.

Work on removing indefinite language from your vocabulary.

When your speech is peppered with "I think," "maybe," "like," and "I guess," not only do you sound unprofessional, but you've made yourself a whole lot less convincing. These words and phrases practically invite others to argue with whatever you're saying. They are not found in the speech of deliberate decision makers. By the time words come out of your mouth, you should be sure enough of them to speak without qualifiers like those listed above. Tune into how often you say these words and try stopping yourself before you do.

Establish a decision-making process.

This is different for everyone. It may include pros and cons lists, writing out potential outcomes, or examining processes from various perspectives. Find what works best for you and keep it in your back pocket at all times. Ideally, you also have a version of this process you can use when decisions need to happen very quickly or even immediately. Stick to this and even your quickest decisions will be good ones.

Reflect on past decisions.

After making a decision and following through on it, take a moment to reflect on how it worked out for everyone involved. This is especially effective for those quick decisions. Keep in mind that this action step is not about ruminating on what you "coulda shoulda woulda" done, but about recognizing how your process worked well and how it could have been better.

CHAPTER 7

CONSISTENCY IS KEY

"It was accountability that Nixon feared." — Bob Woodward

THOUGH THIS IS A RELATIVELY short chapter, consistency is an important topic that I'd like to cover as it's a fundamental of property leadership.

If you remember, fear is a tool that I use to mitigate risk. In the same way, I also use consistency as a tool.

Consistency is more than just doing the same thing all the time. Consistency means that your tenants know what to expect. It means that you don't need to think as much when things go sideways. Finally, it means that when you end up in court, you don't look like a fool because not only will it be easy to remember your clear, consistent patterns, but it'll also show that you have a rock-solid track record.

What if you went to a restaurant with your significant

other and you ordered the same dish, but one came out wrong or different? It would not only be upsetting, but you also wouldn't know what to expect next time.

Tenants, just like anyone, need consistency from their landlords. How do you think a tenant would react if something you punish them for, you didn't punish someone else for a week prior? It can easily look like you're playing favorites, and that's the last thing you want to come up if you end up in court.

It's much easier to tell a judge, "Your honor, I know that I handled this situation a specific way because I handle every tenant situation this way." Remember the candle wax in the carpet from an earlier chapter? Had that gone to court, I could easily say and prove that I always have the carpet professionally handled after a tenant leaves and that I always take photos before the next one moves in.

Having clear and consistent processes in your business will protect you from equal opportunity and discrimination claims as well.

It may not seem obvious to you right away as a new or relatively new landlord. However, one time when it's incredibly important to remain consistent is while showing units to tenants. It's best to decide prior to accepting applications, what your criteria are. If you don't want pets, then no pets for anyone you interview. If you say smokers are okay, then you should probably be consistent throughout the building. You can easily open yourself up to claims of sexism and racial profiling as well if you're not consistent in your choices.

When I show units, I have a standard procedure. First, I list the unit. Once the unit is listed, I line up all the viewers in 30-minute increments on the same day. Usually, I let them choose what time slot they want to take but the times never overlap, and I make sure to tell the applicants that it's first-qualified, first-served.

On showing day, I have each person come in, I interview them individually, and I show them the apartment. If they are on the fence about it, I tell them, in no uncertain terms,

---

"If you choose not to apply now, that's okay. I will happily take your application later in the day. However, the unit will be leased to the first person that qualifies and completes the application."

When I tell people this, it serves two purposes. First, it makes it clear that I'm not going to choose someone else over them based on anything other than the fact that they were interested in the apartment and passed the application. Second, it adds a little pressure to help push wishy-washy people over the fence. It weeds out folks who probably aren't actually interested.

If you have trouble being consistent, try writing down your procedures. Record them in a word document or a notebook. When difficult situations arise, before you act, read your rules and consider how they apply to the situation at hand. If it's something new, then create a new procedure. Simple things like this could be the difference between winning in court or looking like a tool.

This brings me to my next point. It may seem like an

obvious one, but enough landlords try to skip out on it that I had to include it.

Keep Good Records

Just do it. It's tedious and boring, and sometimes you'll never look at them again, but it can save your ass when dealing with precarious situations or difficult clients. So suck it up and develop a solid system of record-keeping that you use ALL THE TIME. See how I tied in consistency there? These two practices go hand in hand. Employ both of them, and you'll be in good shape.

When I was a police officer in the Army, keeping good records was drilled into my mind, and for a good reason. If you do hard and honest work, you don't want a lapse in paperwork to complicate things for you. I quickly learned the importance of documenting all kinds of information:

- Conversations
- Agreements
- Leases
- Payments

Keeping good records is paramount to running a healthy business, and this IS a business. It doesn't matter if you're living in an apartment and own zero units or have 1000 units. Run your finances like a business.

If you don't keep good records, you'll be unable to

- Sue contractors
- Evict tenants

- Prove that you're not discriminating
- Determine your profit (or lack thereof)
- Itemize your taxes (this is HUGE)

Pretty compelling reasons, I'd say. And the only reasons not to keep good records?

- You're hiding something
- You're lazy

You can decide for yourself which reasons are important to you.

Developing an optimal record-keeping system that suits your work and organization style can take time. If you haven't yet learned the ins and outs of the business, it'll be tough to know where to begin and exactly what all needs to be recorded. Over time, if you're smart, you'll figure out the best ways to record, store, and utilize data to support you and your business. For now, here are some general guidelines and information about the systems I have in place.

1. Take photos of each unit immediately before a new tenant arrives and immediately after one leaves. Be sure to time-stamp the photos.
2. Keep copies of each of your receipts—from stores, contractors, or for payments from your tenants. Have a designated place to keep these receipts so that it becomes a habit to put them there whenever you get them. Organize them neatly, so you always have them should you

need them, such as when tax time comes. As a
business owner, many expenses related to your
business may be tax-deductible, so staying
organized in this way will save you money!

3. Have a folder for the tenants of each unit. Take
   note of any issues that come up and date them
   so that you have a list to refer to should the
   situation go south. You can also take this a step
   further and note things you'd like to remember,
   like their dog's name or a birthday, so that you
   can mention them when the time comes up.
   This is a great way to foster professional
   relationships.

4. Have a backup of any digital records. This is
   important for anyone, but especially for
   business owners. Invest in an external hard
   drive or OneDrive to ensure that even in the
   case of a flood or drop or failing computer,
   you'll have all the information you need. Have
   a set time every week that you backup
   everything.

5. Trust no one. It sounds harsh, but it has saved
   me more times than I can count. Treat
   everyone you do business with as if they've
   already burned you. In terms of contractors,
   that means you should get ALL deals in
   writing, you should get second opinions on any
   major maintenance work before signing off on
   it, and you should take photos before and after
   any work is done. For tenants, background
   checks are essential. Never hand off the keys

until the deposit and first month's rent are paid in full, and, again, take those photos before move-in and post move-out.

6. Wear a decent body cam. You can get inexpensive, law-enforcement-grade versions from Amazon.

7. OneNote is an excellent place to store everything related to your rentals because it's easy to upload to and it syncs across all of your devices. I use OneNote to record receipts, photos of damage, work that needs to be done for each property, conversations, and more.

8. This one is based on your state laws, but in Ohio it's okay to record phone calls. I use a phone call recording app on my phone. You never know when a tenant is going to spring something on you and it's extraordinarily helpful to have a recorded call of them admitting guilt when you go to court.

If you still aren't convinced that excellent record keeping is an essential aspect of your business, perhaps these first-hand accounts will sway you.

The first involves the worst contractor I've ever worked with. It was for a big project—a roof repair, and the work was beyond what I was familiar with. But this guy didn't have me convinced he could do it either. Red flag after red flag came up early in the process of working with him. He wouldn't provide or agree to a real contract. He didn't want to solidify and list start and end dates for the project. He was *very* agreeable to all of my requests, to the point where I was suspicious, to say the least.

Well, as it turned out, the guy was just the scumbag he appeared to be. He did only half the work he was contracted to do, and that work was so subpar it could hardly count.

Knowing I had a potentially tricky situation on my hands, I hired multiple inspectors to check out the roof to make sure I was right. I made sure the guys I hired this time knew their stuff, even calling the local roofing supply company and getting the best flat top roofer around to come to inspect the work.

Once they did that, I confronted the original contractor about the shoddy work. When he refused to refund me any of the repair costs, I sued, knowing I had the stronger case.

The magistrate was clear that the onus was on me to prove that the scumbag contractor had done as bad a job as I claimed he did. Now, as a nonprofessional in the roofing industry, there's only so much I could have argued with just photos to back me up.

Enter my expert witness, the best roofer from the roofing supply company, there to tear the contractor to shreds with his testimony. He explained exactly what the contractor had done wrong and proved that the work was insufficient with his evident expertise.

Without him as a witness, I would have lost the case and been stuck with a damaged roof and no refund. But the expert testimony and the pristine records I'd kept meant that things worked out in my favor without too much stress on my part.

This next tale involves my very first tenant.

Unfortunately, this tenant chose to try me when I was fresh out of the Army and in very little mood to deal with any bullshit.

Here's how it went. I made the rookie mistake of letting this tenant pay just half the deposit up front and the rest within the first month of moving in. I also gave them the keys before confirming their payment or that the utilities were in their name. Not the best moves, I know, but hey, I was new.

The tenants left the utilities in my name and never paid. I filed for eviction, no questions asked. And here's the thing, even though I made these mistakes, the records I kept saved the day. I had copies of the lease agreement and the payments the tenant hadn't made. The magistrate looked over all of this and promptly gave the tenant two weeks to vacate and required him to pay the utility bills he'd left in my name.

I learned my lesson, that's for sure. Now I never give a tenant keys until all of the move-in requirements are met. Without exception, I do background checks on every single tenant before the lease is signed. And I keep excellent records of everything, knowing that even if I slip up somewhere, they'll back me up.

CHAPTER 8

KNOW YOUR STUFF

"Any fool can know. The point is to understand" —
Albert Einstein

I'VE ALREADY ESTABLISHED THAT, as a landlord,
you run a business. In business, there are almost always
people looking to take advantage of you. Sometimes they
do so subconsciously, sometimes it's pretty intentional, but
the risk is always there. Tenants, real estate agents, and
contractors may all look for nicks in your armor that allow
them to strike.

The best defense against this is to minimize nicks. And
how do you do that?

You have to know your stuff.

Think about it. Sports teams win by attacking the
defense's physical weak points. Bullies make their impact
by attacking their victims' emotional weak points. Those in

the business world win court cases and deals by attacking others' figurative weak points, their areas of non-expertise. They bet and prey on what they assume the other doesn't know or hasn't taken care of.

If they think you're new to the game, realtors will try to hide a property's fatal flaws from you. If they think you have no clue what landscaping or a roof repair should cost, you can bet contractors will overcharge you. And of course, if they believe you're new to the area or out of touch with the local scene, tenants will try like hell to push rent down. If you've done your research, you'll see past all of these phonies easily. If you don't know the laws at play in this business, any of these threats can pull you down fast.

I definitely fell victim to this early on in my experience as a landlord.

A tenant—let's call her Jessica—was inherited with a building I bought and took over. Soon after meeting her, it became clear to me that she was very emotionally unstable. She took almost all of our interactions to extremes and had more outbursts than I could count. On more than one occasion, I witnessed her crying for no discernable reason.

She also complained about everything. Despite paying far below market value for rent, she complained about the lack of a free washer and dryer in the building and about how the snow removal company put a whopping two inches of snow behind her car. She was also known to park her car in the middle of the lot, preventing anyone from getting in or out.

She was impossible to please. She'd call me about needing work done in her apartment, so I'd send a contractor over and let her know the time he'd be around.

She refused this, saying that she would be at work and didn't want him in her apartment while she wasn't there. When I went along with this and set up an appointment for the contractor to come on the weekend, she refused to let him in because she couldn't be bothered while she was relaxing. How she expected this work to get done, if not during the week or on the weekend, is beyond me.

On top of the inconvenience of being such a difficult tenant, she was paying just $200 per month in rent. Based on the market value of her unit, that was about $450 too low. I had no choice but to raise the rent to avoid losing money on the building, but I wasn't trying to kick anyone out. I go out of my way to avoid evicting people, so even though Jessica was difficult, I tried to make things work.

I talked to her about adjusting the rent after I took over the building. She immediately retaliated, saying that the price I was asking for, which was market value, was absurd and that I'd never get it. Apparently, she was an expert landlord herself (can you hear my sarcasm?) because she tried to tell me that most property owners lose money on investments. Okay, sure. Unfortunately, this isn't the only time I've had a tenant straight out lie to me to get their way somehow. The only way to be prepared for situations like this is to have as much knowledge in your back pocket as possible.

Still, I wasn't trying to get rid of her; I just wanted to get her to pay a fair price for the unit. But she refused, so I found someone else to rent out the apartment and looked forward to the day she'd be out of my hair.

In the last few days of her lease, however, she suddenly changed her tune. She begged me to let her stay. Of course, at that point, even if she offered me what I'd asked for, I legally couldn't let her stay because I had new tenants waiting to take it over.

So Jessica would have to find a new place to live. But of course, she didn't leave it at that. She had the nerve to list me as a reference for her next apartment.

I didn't know this until that property manager called me. I answered all of her questions honestly, without ever alluding to the idea that Jessica was an absolute nightmare to deal with. While she'd been a hassle, I didn't want to be the guy to throw someone under the bus out of spite. And everyone needs a place to live, after all.

However, at the very end of the conversation, the property manager asked if I would ever rent to this woman again.

"Heck no," I said, still being utterly honest. When the property manager asked, I explained why, calmly and rationally.

I highly doubt that Jessica got that apartment.

While this whole situation was ultimately worked out —Jessica found somewhere to go, the maintenance to the unit was completed, and the new tenants paid market value rent—I could have saved myself a whole lot of hassle if I'd had a better grip on landlord-tenant laws.

Disputes like this will vary depending on the area, but my locale is set up to help landlords who follow the rules. Had I known the laws back then, I would have known that Jessica did not have the right to refuse my contractor from coming in, whether she was there or not.

Knowing the laws that govern landlords and tenants in one's area can make or break a landlord. And to be honest, the information isn't very difficult to find. There's a lot of it, for sure, but it's by no means hidden, and in a lot of cases, it's even free. If I had to recommend a place to start, it would be as simple as this:

Since each state has its own set of tenant-landlord laws, begin by Googling "<your state> Tenant Landlord Laws. " What you find there is what judges will use as foundational principles in all court cases. If you follow those laws to the letter, you'll be fine.

Like these, almost all of the tools I use and have used in my property management education are free. There are countless resources out there, covering everything from the very basics to the minutiae of being a landlord. All of this readily available information means that there is absolutely no excuse not to know your stuff. Read up, or expect to pay up.

There is also a massive online community for landlords and real estate investors. When I was first starting, most of my education came from various forums and from Youtube. These resources continue to serve me and my business on a regular basis. Any time I come up against something I don't know how to deal with, which happens frequently, I turn first to Google, doing a general search to see if I can find an answer quickly. If I'm not successful there, then I turn to Youtube, where people from all over are eager to share their knowledge. Youtube can teach you a world of skills and information, and it costs nothing. And yet, if after looking there, I still can't find what I'm looking for, then I hone in on the real estate investing community and turn to industry-specific forums to see if anyone has encountered the same issue I'm facing. If no one has asked the question yet, I'll post an inquiry myself, give it 15 minutes to bake, and I'm bound to have ten answers waiting for me.

Don't let your education stop with the basics, though. I've seen far too many landlords flounder because they've never bothered to research the rules surrounding some more specific situations. They get themselves stuck because they have no clue about things like the Americans with Disabilities Act. This is where you open yourself up to lawsuits, and that's not a path you want to go down.

For example, I've seen plenty of landlords put in their ads that they do not allow dogs in their units and specify that that includes service dogs. If they'd done any research, those amateur landlords would know that this is a lawsuit waiting to happen. As someone with a service dog myself, I can tell you that anyone with a legitimate service dog knows where to find the Fair Housing Act and ADA laws and is well aware of what those laws entitle them to. Stay a step ahead by reading up on things like this before they become an issue.

I've had tenants pressure me on the legality of decisions more than once. It's crucial to remain calm in these situations. It's also imperative that you know your local tenant-landlord laws, state laws, and what's in your lease, as I discussed in the last chapter. If you're not confident that you're following the law and lease, these tenants will detect this, and they will push that button until they get the results they want.

I distinctly remember a simple issue I had with a tenant a few years back. The tenants were a husband and wife with two children who lived in a three-bedroom apartment of mine. These tenants were acquired with the property and hadn't gone through my strict filtering policies, so I had no sense or control of whether they were decent or not. I always let tenants let me down, though. I never prematurely kick someone out just because they were there when I took the building over. You never know what quality of tenant someone is just based on their previous landlord. Just like you never know about an employee or soldier you acquired from a previous leader. There could have been personality conflicts. The previous leader could have been a schmuck. There's a number of possibilities. When I take over a new building and onboard existing tenants, I give them clear expectations, and I give them enough rope to hang themselves. If they want to stay on as a tenant, they'll do what I expect from all my tenants. If they fail to meet the standards, then they get ousted, and I replace them with a high-quality, vetted tenant.

So, I told these tenants that I had acquired what the expectations were. I told them when rent was due, how to pay it and what the consequences were for not meeting this standard. After a couple of months, they started to be a day late. Then two days late.

This was the first time I had encountered tenants with children that would push the limits like this, so I was hesitant to evict them right away. After the six-month mark of their lease, I had to make a decision. I decided that they weren't the quality of tenants I wanted to keep on board, so I gave them six months' notice that they would be expected to leave at the end of their lease. There was no arguing or push back. The tenants acknowledged that they would leave at the end of their lease, and things continued as normal. The tenants would leave at the end of December when their lease expired.

On December 1ˢᵗ, I went to the property to collect rent from the tenants. This predated my all-electronic rental system, so I had to do this in person. There was a moving truck outside. The tenants that were expected to leave were doing so a month early. I went to speak with them.

They told me they would be out by the end of the day, and I reminded them that rent was due for that month. The lease clearly stated that they were required to pay to the end of the lease unless they gave me 60 days' notice that they were leaving early. They just said "okay," and I left them alone so they could continue to move.

The next day, I contacted them for the rent, and they told me that they left, so they weren't paying. I once again reminded them of their obligation to the lease, but they essentially told me to pound sand. It was at this point that I had to make a choice. Should I take them to court for the missing rent from last month, or just garnish the security deposit? There wasn't really any damage to the apartment, and I had been planning on a full rehab of it anyhow, so I decided that it wasn't worth chasing them. I would just take the security deposit and be done with it.

Once I informed the tenants that they wouldn't get their deposit back, I heard every legal term you could imagine. They threatened me with lawyers, the wife told me her sister was a police officer, they told me I would lose everything, and the list went on. Since I was well versed in the tenant-landlord laws, I knew that the law was almost certainly on my side, so I recognized how hollow their threats were, and I wasn't worried. It's been years since this happened, and I'm still waiting for my court summons about that deposit.

You can't be afraid when a tenant starts throwing around legal jargon. You certainly don't want to start a discussion with them if you're unsure of the law. This goes back to being confident when you speak. I don't think I would recommend telling a tenant you don't know the law, but be honest with yourself, at least. If you're unsure of something a tenant is threatening you with, stop the conversation, and figure out the answer before you say and or do something that will put you in a corner. It's been my experience with the courts that they are very reasonable. If you have a contract and follow the contract, and the contract doesn't violate the law, you're going to be okay. The key here is knowing what you're required to do, what you're allowed to do, and what the tenant must do. This should all be documented in your local state tenant-landlord laws. If there's any question, call an attorney. Many cities often have free tenant-landlord services set up to help mediate issues.

Policies honestly don't change all that often in the rental business, so put in the work to learn your stuff at the beginning and save yourself lots of hassle later. Besides that, just keep your eyes and ears open to any unusual changes that might occur, such as the eviction moratorium that occurred during the COVID-19 pandemic.

To make sure you have your bases covered when it comes to knowing the laws, make sure you look into the following:

. . .

The Fair Housing Act

This covers the bare minimum policies against discrimination regarding accepting tenants.

The Fair Credit Reporting Act

It's important to screen tenants' credit before accepting them, but certain laws apply if you decide to reject them based on this information. Make sure that you know these.

The Implied Warranty of Inhabitability

This shouldn't have to be a rule, but the world has enough scumbags in it to make it necessary. This rule describes the bare minimum of what a landlord must maintain for a residence to be habitable and what rights tenants have if it isn't.

Rules of Privacy/Entry

These let you know exactly what you need to do to enter an occupied unit legally.

Eviction regulations

These let you know explicitly how to handle evictions to ensure you are in the clear legally.

Security deposit regulations

These tend to vary between states, so check out the specifics of what you can and cannot do regarding a tenant's security deposit.

General landlord/tenant laws

These can also vary significantly by state, so do your research to find specifics.

Not only will this self-education and diligence leave you less susceptible to poor characters and lawsuits, but it will also bolster all of the other attributes this book advocates for. When you have all the information, you'll be far better equipped to put your tenants first because you'll know exactly what their rights are and how they intertwine with yours. You'll be well-prepared to command respect and lead with calm self-assurance because you'll know exactly what you're dealing with. You'll be able to be deliberate and decisive in the face of any situation because you'll have all the information necessary to make responsible and legal decisions. And with this knowledge, you'll develop systems that consistently make your tenants happy and your business a success.

CHAPTER 9

I DON'T KNOW

"And if I claim to be a wise man, it surely means that I don't know." – Kansas

---

IT'S tough when people look to you for answers. It's not always easy being the go-to source of information. The military has taught me many valuable lessons that I carry with me in life, but one of the most valuable is enforcing that it's okay to say, "I don't know."

Being a military leader is often high stakes.

Wrong decisions can cost you and others their lives.

Wrong decisions can destroy families of non-combatants.

Wrong decisions can cause international incidents.

When making decisions in combat, you need to not only be decisive, but you need to know when to say, "I don't know." If you can't say that, then you're not humble enough to lead, and you need to step down.

The same is true in business. You may not have to worry about someone being killed by a bad business decision, but missteps can still be catastrophic. If you can't say "I don't know," then you're not ready.

Humility is an important quality in any leader. The great leaders of the world know that the people around them are the cornerstones of all decisions. As a soon-to-be-great leader yourself, you need to be able to ask for help when you need it. You need to be able to look at the people around you and recognize their wisdom, regardless of what area of expertise it might be.

If you do it right, you will come across as honest, trustworthy, humble, and respectful. Leaders who can't ask for help or can't say "I don't know" on occasion are perceived as arrogant. Worse, if you make a decision that your subordinates don't think you fully thought out, they'll lose confidence in you. Once your team loses confidence, you'll have a hell of a time regaining it.

A team's confidence in one another is essential. If a team doesn't have confidence in each other to make the right choice, then instead of focusing on their job, they'll be focusing on the person next to them, questioning internally (or maybe even vocally) if they're making the right choice. When they question their leader, they may not say it out loud, but it runs through their minds. Once this starts, it's as if the entire team has consumed a cup of poison. The leader loses all credibility if it's not fixed.

The Army was great at weeding out people who weren't ready. Sometimes we had ill-prepared people slip through, and they were brutal to deal with, but for the most part, the leaders I had were outstanding. The way the military accomplished this was by putting them through a series of tests. Through these, we needed to prove that we had the knowledge, the strength, and the will to earn our stripes. At the end of it, there was a promotion board made up of all our senior leadership. We sat in front of this board for around 30 minutes, wearing dress uniforms that were inspected for the most minute details. We would be expected to sit at the position of attention, feet about a foot apart and flat on the ground, hands on legs, fingers straight, back straight, and head angled to speak to the person asking the questions.

The questions in the promotion board weren't easy either. I distinctly remember filling out hundreds of note cards with questions on one side and answers on the other, memorizing every detail verbatim.

"What is the cyclic rate of an M249 automatic machine gun?"

"How do you call for a nine-line medivac on the radio?"

"What are the signs of shock in a victim?"

"What is the effective range of an M2?"

The senior leaders would listen to the way you answered each question. They would listen for certain inflections in your voice, signaling any lack of confidence in your answer. If they detected it, they would drill in to gauge your understanding and push you to say, "I don't know."

I was always told it's okay to say "I don't know," as long as you add that you know where to find the answer and that you'll get that answer and return it to them after the board meeting. Lord help you if you didn't follow up.

These leaders wanted to make sure that whomever they gave responsibility to could handle intense pressure. If you can't handle a few questions from some people that outrank you, then how could you handle young soldiers looking up to you for answers in the pressures of combat.

As mentioned earlier, the same is true in business. It's okay to say, "I don't know." Make sure you find the answer, though. If a tenant is inquiring about something, and you leave them without an answer, it comes across as unprofessional. It also smacks of incompetence. If you can get an answer and deliver it to the tenant confidently, you position yourself as a truthful, reliable source of information.

Another point that I'd like to highlight in the vein of being considered competent is that if your tenants think you're incompetent, they're more likely to push the limits. For example, if your tenants ask you a question about the law, which the crafty ones will do from time to time to gauge your understanding, and you give a bullshit answer, then they'll smell blood in the water. As soon as they have an opportunity to pull on that lever, they're going to do it. Always remain professional, and always do your best to appear competent. You'll save yourself a ton of headaches down the line. I don't recommend giving legal advice to tenants, though. Always point them to an attorney if they start going down that road. However, don't shy away when you're accused of breaking the law. Make it clear you follow the tenant-landlord laws and the lease to the letter.

Saying "I don't know" has uses outside of rentals, too.

No one likes a yes person. Real leaders making real business decisions, definitely don't. They want someone that they can go to for an honest answer. Now, I have a no-filter personality. I'm not sure if I was born this way or if I developed this personality in the military, but if you ask me a question, you're going to get an honest answer or an "I don't know." For better or worse, if I think a product or a decision is shit, I say so. One of two things will happen. Either the leadership will ask why and determine if my point is valid, or they'll expand on the product or decision so that I can get on board. You know one thing that's never happened, though? I've never been punished for being an honest, no-filter type of person. This leads me to believe that leadership respects honest personalities. Sure, I can be abrasive at times with this personality, but abrasiveness can be smoothed out. You know what you can't smooth out? A person you can't trust. Those people just get ignored and/or let go. So don't be a yes person. Just be honest, or say, "I don't know, but I can get you the answer." You'll be much better off for it.

CHAPTER 10

GOAL SETTING AND FAILURES

"Only those who dare to fail greatly can ever achieve greatly." — Robert F. Kennedy

---

MANY PEOPLE SEEM to be under the impression that property leading is a "one step to success" sort of situation. They think that all they need to do is purchase a property, find tenants, and let the money pour in each month. This is a common misconception that results from the very nature of the business, and these two factors especially:

1. **Most people interact with their landlords only when money is involved.**

That is, whenever rent comes due or they need something fixed and want their landlord to pay for it. The vast majority of tenants don't have any exposure to the backend work that landlords must do in order to run an ethical and profitable business.

2. **Many landlords treat their businesses this way.**

The good ones don't, but unfortunately, many others do. They make themselves scarce anytime they aren't collecting money. They don't check in on their tenants, and they don't reach out personally when issues arise. They hide out and hope for the best, essentially.

Hopefully, if you've read up to this point, you no longer subscribe to this idea. For a good landlord, a landlord who is a Property Leader, the idea that renting out property is an easy way to get rich quickly could not be further from the truth. Good landlording is a complex and multifaceted pursuit built on solid relationships, excellent communication, and thorough diligence. And as with all such pursuits, a plan is essential for landlording success. Landlords steer the ship. That means they need to know what direction they're headed in, and that requires goals.

GOAL SETTING

The military strongly emphasizes goal setting. From basic training on up, I was pushed to set goals for myself and work consistently to reach them. These goals were usually related to one of two things: weight loss or fitness. We would set goals to lose a certain amount of weight within a particular time period or shave seconds off a mile time within a certain number of weeks. We were responsible for setting these goals and determining how to reach them. This impulse sticks with me in everything I do. I can use it to lose weight reliably and efficiently or to boost my income enough to pay off a purchase or acquire a new property. While it's not foolproof, I can be sure that even if I do not achieve my precise goal, I will have gotten fairly close.

Goals allow you to look both at the big picture and the minutiae of your business, and that combination is where success lives. So let's break down how you can set goals for your landlording business. The two most important questions to consider are as follows:

1. **Is it measurable?**
2. **Is it time-based?**

These two questions are what will separate you and your thriving business from the millions of New Year's Resolutions that go unfulfilled each year. Goals that can't answer positively to these two questions have a meager chance of success.

The first ensures that you have a means of evaluating whether or not you achieved your goal, and the second ensures that you have a set time to assess it. Just saying you want to "get healthier" or even "lose some weight" is not a measurable goal. The first example is rather subjective, while with the second, you can lose a single pound and technically have achieved your goal, but I guarantee you won't feel all that much different. Plus, you won't have any predetermined time to evaluate your progress, so you'll do it when you feel good and shy away from it when you don't, and that is nothing but another avoidance tactic.

Harsh, but true. This strategy does not support long-term success. You need to give yourself concrete statistics to look at to evaluate your progress, and for that, you need goals that include measurable data and deadlines. For example, "I am going to bring my blood pressure down to 120/80 within one year from today," or "I am going to lose 30 pounds in three months."

It's important to note that one of these things cannot make you successful without the other. Think about it. You can say that you want to lose 10 pounds, but until you put an end date on that goal (i.e., I want to lose 10 pounds in 3 months), there's no way to determine if you've succeeded or not because you allow yourself the ever-present excuse of "I'll start Monday" or "I just haven't done it *yet.*"

Measurable and time-based goal setting is what really allows you to demystify your goals. "Losing weight" or "achieving financial freedom" may be great ideas for you to pursue, but they're rather daunting. That's because they're unclear and, therefore, difficult to break down. You can't tell me precisely what you need to do each week to reach those goals because they are not in specific terms. When you make them measurable and time-based, you can break them down into definite steps with results that can be easily evaluated. For example, if you decide on the goal of losing 10 pounds in 3 months, you can break that down into exactly how much exercise you'll need to do or how many calories you'll need to consume each day. If your goal is to make $100K this year, you can determine how much you'll need to make each month or divide 100,000 by your hourly rate to determine how many hours you'll need to work. Measurable and time-based goals are powerful because they simplify big pursuits into simple math. Without them, you are left with a vague idea that you should move more and eat less or work more and spend less, but no clarity on what that looks like.

Goals like this are psychologically beneficial as well. They allow you the satisfaction of knowing when you are fulfilling those requirements. That reinforces the positive behaviors you're trying to develop and makes the continual pursuit of your goal easier. Imagine how much better about yourself and your progress you will feel if you hit benchmarks each day, week, or month. This works for health goals, financial goals, and business goals alike because it's all about watching the small things add up.

This process also works both for big picture and more specific situations, and, perhaps most importantly, it allows for adjustments along the way. I started small with my goals at the beginning of my real estate investing journey. At first, I aimed only to break even with my investments. I planned accordingly, determining how much I would need to charge for each unit in order to cover my mortgage payments and any maintenance for the building. Once I achieved that, I aimed to cover my basic expenses as well. I took note of exactly what each of these expenses was and their total when I set this goal so that I could invest in and price units accordingly. Once I achieved that, I moved on to do all of the above plus give myself a specified amount of spending money. Achieving each of these goals reinforced my positive habits and showed me just how much was possible in the real estate business. I soon realized that I'd be able to replace my full-time income with my real estate business. I determined exactly what I would need to make each month and devised a strategy accordingly. As you may have noticed, strategic goal setting is always a matter of looking at what you want and working backward from there.

If you're a landlord just starting out and you're not sure what your goal breakdowns should look like, I encourage you to try something along these lines:

Make a net profit of X within a month of acquiring the building.

- *Before purchasing your rental, determine what you believe your expenses will be. There's a litany of examples out there, but I will provide a simple breakdown of expenses at the end of this chapter.*
- *Use free online tools to gauge the rent in the area you wish to purchase with comparable apartments to the ones you're considering.*
- *Determine if, with all expenses, the rent will at least cover your cost. If it doesn't, it's a red flag that the property is overvalued for you. You can use this as a tool to work the asking price down or explore more creative financing options to make the numbers work.*
- *The goal is not just to break even, though, so you should then factor in how much you want to earn per door per month. Personally, I won't even look at a building if I know I won't be able to net at least $250 per door per month.*

FAILURE

Before we get into the nitty-gritty, let me just say that if you're setting goals, you're already doing far better than many, many landlords. That is because so many fail to set goals at all out of fear they won't reach them. If you're thinking like this, then you need to seriously reevaluate. Those who hide from failure also hide from success.

Failure is just as critical as success in business and in life. That's because failure is where you learn your lessons. It's just part of human nature. Look at the way kids learn to walk and eat and dress themselves. They mess it up a few times, maybe stumble, end up with food all over their faces, or put their shirts on inside out. And they realize it's wrong and don't do it again the next time. They don't stop trying to learn. If they did, we'd have a whole lot of messy, poorly-dressed people crawling around.

In the military, too, failure is nothing but a jumping-off point. Failure cannot simply be accepted because that's not how combat works. You can't just get someone to come bail you out when you've gotten yourself into a difficult place. If you make a mistake and wind up injured or stranded, you have to find a way to move forward, to evaluate your situation, and decide on your next move.

Somehow this gets a little messy when it comes to adults trying to learn from their mistakes, but it doesn't have to. All you really need to do is be honest with yourself. As soon as something is wrong, ask yourself these questions to nip it in the bud.

- What went wrong?
- Why did it go wrong?
- How will you avoid the same thing happening in the future?
- What's your next best move?

Keep track of your answers to these questions because that's how you learn from your mistakes.

And if you've gotten this far, I'll let you in on a little secret: catastrophic losses are not the norm. They're the exception. So when you fear losing every dollar to your name in an investment or being sued for all you're worth, you're fearing something with a probability so low it's not worth the time it takes to type it. When you set effective goals and pursue them responsibly, then even if you don't meet the precise quotas you set for yourself, you'll be doing better than most. Personally, I don't fail as much as I used to, and that's because of the goal systems I've put in place. These systems are so airtight that even when everything that could go wrong does, I am still profitable. This is all because of carefully thought-out goals. I don't say this to brag or boast. I say this so that perhaps you will let go of some of that fear of failure and see what is possible.

COMPONENTS TO CONSIDER WHEN GAUGING MONTHLY EXPENSES

- Monthly mortgage payment (broken down by principal, interest, insurance, and taxes because someday it'll be paid off, but you'll still need to pay insurance and taxes)
- Utilities that the landlord must cover
- Landscaping (usually only a few months of the year, so take the total estimated amount and divide by 12 to spread the cost out)
- Snow removal (usually only a few months of the year, so take the total estimated amount and divide by 12 to spread the cost out)
- 15% of gross rent should be reserved for capital expenditures (things that need to be repaired regularly that we estimate for)
- Note that in some cities, there are rental licensing fees. The cost is dependent on your city, but mine average to around $45 per unit per year.
- Also, all of this is tax-deductible, so make sure you keep good records!

CHAPTER 11

LEARN FROM FAILURE

"If you fail to plan, you're planning to fail" —
Benjamin Franklin

AS I DISCUSSED in the last chapter, many landlords refrain from setting goals because they are afraid to fail at them. They would rather bury their heads in the sand than face the fact that they don't measure up. Property Leaders, however, recognize that this is a major loss of potential. They know that whether or not they reach their goals, opportunities for growth abound. They know how to learn from failure.

First, let's just get this straight. It is OKAY to fail. Many of us grew up in school systems that told us failing was the worst-case scenario, that it was to be avoided at all costs and that it wouldn't happen if we tried our best. As adults, it's time for us all to realize that that is not the case.

It's okay to fall short of your goals, to mess up in a major way, and to falter in the face of something important. It may not feel great in the moment, but I can promise you that it won't kill you, and will, indeed, make you stronger. And in a way, it's like getting in your veggies. It doesn't always taste good, but without it, your body won't grow. If you aren't failing, you probably aren't trying anything new. You're staying still instead of moving forward, and you almost definitely aren't learning.

Popular wisdom says that the way to avoid failure is to try your best. Supposedly, if you do your best, you'll have nothing else to worry about. But in order to make real progress in this complicated world, we've got to take into account the fact that even if you give something your absolute best shot, try everything you can and do everything by the book, you could still fail. Life, and business especially, isn't a video game. You can't just ensure success with the right combinations of buttons pressed. Not everything is within your control, which is just another reason why it's so important to accept failure as part of the job. If you can't control everything, you can't blame yourself for everything. All you can do is take responsibility for what is your doing, acknowledge what went wrong, and decide the best way to move forward. If you work in this way, failure can be the best teacher you'll ever have. You just have to listen to what it says.

I've given you lots of examples in this book of less-than-great tenants. Drunk tenants, tenants who act like children, and tenants that try and take advantage of anything they can. The key takeaway from all these stories is that in each one, my mistake was different. No two stories turn sour because of the same mistake. That is because I am determined to take the lessons learned from each mistake I make and apply them to my business. I don't let them break my determination or push me away from real estate investing. I learned from my mistakes and quickly grew as a leader so that I wouldn't make them again

As Grant Cardone says, don't be a little bitch. My interpretation of this is don't curl up and quit when things get tough. Pick yourself up by your bootstraps and keep going.

Another point that I think way too many people miss, especially at the beginning of their real estate investing ventures, is that you don't have to wait for your own failures to learn some valuable lessons. You can learn from other people's mistakes. As I said early on in this book, if you aren't able to follow, you'll never be able to lead. So make it a point to read about what other people are experiencing—either in books or online—and add that to your mental catalog. Follow along on online forums to see how other people deal with problems that you may well face soon. Either they will get around those things successfully and you can learn from what they did, or they will fail, and you can learn from that, too. It doesn't cost you anything and you can do it on your own time.

Sometimes you can even reach out and message them to find out how they handle certain things. If you're in a difficult situation, post a question in a forum or reach out to a leader in the field to see if they have any advice. Always filter responses through your personal judgement, of course, because not everything on the internet will be in your best interest, but it's worth weeding through the bad answers to get some insight that might be useful for you. There's a wealth of resources and a rich community of true leaders out there. Use this to your advantage.

I've been saved countless times by my peers letting me know about a particular law I may have otherwise missed. If I hadn't been proactive enough to ask questions before I failed, I would have ended up in a tough spot.

Some people feel hesitant about reaching out to others, especially to individuals. I think there's this idea out there that being a landlord is a solitary pursuit and one must do it all on their own. This couldn't be further from the truth, and we would all do well to dispel this myth. Landlords don't exist in a vacuum after all. We depend on each other to share experiences, set standards, and promote best practices. And that teamwork is out there; you just have to look for it. There is a rich community of landlords out there just desperate to share their knowledge with others. Take this book, for example.

Like all those at the top of their fields, landlords worth their salt will want to help boost others up, not tear them down. There are countless people on forums and in online communities who are ready and willing to mentor newcomers to the business, and I encourage anyone feeling unsure about their knowledge to pursue this. It is the most direct and often most fruitful way to learn from the mistakes of others.

CHAPTER 12

LEADING THROUGH CRISIS

---

*"The ideal man bears the accidents of life with
dignity and grace, making the best of
circumstances" — Aristotle*

THROUGHOUT THIS BOOK, I've done my best to
show that being a landlord requires incredible fortitude
and real strength of character. There's far more to it than
finding tenants and cashing rent checks. Being a Property
Leader, likewise, is much deeper than barking orders. So
what does Property Leading really boil down to?

At its core, leadership is about empathy. Without that,
you can be a manager at best, but never a leader. Being a
leader as a landlord means understanding that you're
dealing with the lives of real people. You must keep in
mind that you have a degree of control over lives just as full
and complex as your own and act accordingly. Without

this implicit understanding, landlords may behave as if they're playing a game of chess with the lives of others. They can quickly lose sight of the fact that their game pieces are human beings.

Developing a strong sense of empathy, on the other hand, makes communication—real communication—possible. It allows you to inspire empathy in those you lead so that you can make your goal their goal as well. This type of communication allows you to influence someone to take up your mission of their own free will. Nothing is more powerful than a team that can do this, and by building such a team, one becomes truly successful.

Nowhere is this mindset more important than when handling a crisis.

In recent years, the idea of crisis management has become increasingly relevant to all of us, no matter who we are or where we live. Through the pandemic especially, we have seen that no one is immune to the impacts of some crises, regardless of how prepared we are. I will address these major, life-altering crises and guide you to deal with them, but I'd like to first talk about the smaller, everyday crises they are sure to come up sooner rather than later. I want to show you how you can use the same process you use to address a flooded basement to handle the effects of, say, a pandemic.

The bottom line is that no matter how well-prepared, experienced, or organized you are, roofs cave in, water heaters blow and flood basements, mice and cockroaches appear out of nowhere, and furnaces quit at 2 AM on Christmas. The list goes on. You can't control these mishaps.

What you can control is how you handle them. You can choose to be a coward. You can run, hide, and pretend things are fine, or you can choose to handle the situation quickly, safely, and correctly, with the tenant's best interest in mind.

The poor leader will fail to take positive action in situations like these. They will put their needs above the needs of the people they lead. They will ignore the frantic text or phone call and sleep in, delaying dealing with the issue until it's more convenient for them.

This is where empathy–that ability to put yourself in the position of others–comes in. If you were the person with the flooded basement, leaking roof, or freezing apartment, how would you want your landlord to react?

You'd want them to get their butt out of bed, call a contractor, and immediately start taking any action they can to address the problem. You want to preserve your belongings and get back to living your life as quickly as possible. In short, you want your landlord to deal with the issue as if it were happening in his own home.

One stormy autumn morning around 0400, I was just starting my workout when I saw a call come in from a tenant. When I picked up, I was greeted by a frantic voice telling me the last thing you want to hear to start your day. The ceiling in her apartment had caved in under the intense rainfall, and water was pouring in. Good morning, world.

Without missing a step, I dressed, grabbed my toolkit, and was out the door within minutes of the call, full battle rattle and ready to go.

Once I arrived there, I assessed the situation and

assured the tenant that I was there to help. I told them not to worry and that I'd be there until the situation was well under control.

It quickly became clear that an edge of the flat top roof had come loose. In the stormy weather, it had blown upward and now allowed water to pour into the apartment, traveling down the wall and onto the plaster ceiling in the tenant's bedroom. Already, their bed was saturated with rain. It was a nightmare mode scenario.

Once I had assessed the situation and identified all the points of failure in the tenant's ceiling and the roof, I developed a plan of action and began to execute it.

First, I had the tenant remove all her things from the room, giving me a clear space to work. Next, I got a green dumpster bag from the local hardware store, put it outside the window, and started ripping down the ceiling, which needed to be replaced. In the meantime, I also coordinated with a local general contractor, asking him to come to the house, fix the roof, and put a new ceiling up for me.

In the end, the repair cost me about $500, and the total turnaround time was three days. That's three days from the time it started to the time the tenant was putting her items back into the room. Fast turnarounds like this are one of the many, seemingly small practices I employ which keep me on a level far above my competition. My competitors can't or won't offer such quick service, and therefore don't benefit from the trust it builds between my tenants and I.

To help smooth things over with the tenant, I offered to buy her a new mattress. Between that and her brand new ceiling, light fixture, and repaired roof, the tenant was more than happy.

Crisis successfully handled.

This is how a good leader operates. They address the situation immediately, regardless of the time of day or what they're doing when the call or text comes in. A good leader will act quickly to identify the root problem as swiftly and efficiently as possible, prioritize them wisely, and then start executing on fixing them. A good leader will know how to delegate work to others when necessary or more efficient, all while balancing the budget and keeping the tenant informed.

When things go sideways in my world, which they almost certainly do (every few months, in fact), I don't hide from it. I don't tell myself that if I ignore it for a little, it'll work itself out. I don't minimize issues. When things go off the rails, and it feels like the world is ending, I jump into action. These are the moments where I feel I shine the most.

I haven't always had this process down to such a science, though. It took time for me to figure out how to apply the quick-thinking strategies and problem-solving approaches I learned in the military to matters of property management. However, once I realized that tackling a caving ceiling was like many challenges I faced while leading soldiers, everything began to shift. Along the way, I picked up on a few significant ideas that have held true throughout my experiences as a landlord.

Any crisis will surely challenge you at least a bit. You'll be stretched out of your comfort zone and forced to make quick decisions. To do this, you'll need to be disciplined in your process and procedures. If it helps you, make a checklist for dealing with crises, so you aren't left dumbfounded when one arises. Even if this list is just a brief framework of the different factors you want to consider, it can prove immeasurably valuable when conflict strikes, and you have to act with limited information. Your checklist should include the following:

Get yourself to the site.

Just seeing that you are present will do wonders to ease the tenant's concerns in any serious situation. Plus, it will keep them from ever accusing you of not being responsive or addressing problems quickly.

Reassure the tenant.

Let them know that you are taking action to get the situation under control and solve the problem.

Determine the core of the problem.

If there's a leak, where is it coming from? If there's a pest, where is its hideout? Find the core of the issue and begin your attack there.

Call a contractor if necessary.

Get them on the scene too, and take a look at the problem together.

Discuss cost before work begins, but DO NOT PAY IN ADVANCE. Make sure to let any contractors know that you need a quote before they begin working. If not, it can lead to disputes later if the work turns out not to be within your budget. Some contractors will see someone in a tight spot, know they're not in the right mind to make good decisions, and take advantage by asking for money up front and then vanishing.

The only upfront funds you *may* want to provide are material costs. You can roll the dice and fork over this money when the contractor asks, or you can mitigate risk by accompanying them to the store and purchasing the supplies yourself.

Create a hierarchy of your expenses.

In a more widespread emergency like a natural disaster or a pandemic, you're likely to have more than one tenant in need of assistance. Creating a hierarchy of expenses will help you immensely in such cases. Those expenses required to keep people happy and in healthy apartments are mandatory. These include making sure water heaters and furnaces are functional, and windows are in good repair. Appliances can also fall into this category, but only if they break.

The next tier consists of expenses that you can put off for six months to a year. These include painting, replacing carpeting (unless it is essential for flipping a unit), new additions to existing units, and landscaping beyond what is required to avoid city fines. Keeping this hierarchy in mind will help you make effective decisions.

Before a crisis ever arises, there are some things you can put in place that will make it easier to deal with them.

Save up at least three months' worth of expenses in an emergency fund for your business.

Note that second part. You should have an emergency fund set up exclusively for your business so that you aren't covering unexpected expenses from your own pocket. To make this happen, start shoveling any profit you make into an emergency fund as soon as your business is profitable. That way, when tough times arise, and they inevitably do, you'll be prepared.

Consider setting up a couple of credit lines with zero balances.

Hopefully, you'll never have to use them, but having them just in case can give you both some peace of mind and another option if times get tough.

Establish communication channels for an emergency.

When disaster strikes, every moment becomes precious. Buy yourself as much of it as possible by having a mass text or call service set up to get information to your tenants when you need to. Make sure the tenants know about this as soon as it is set up, not just when an emergency comes up. This will keep you from having to figure out how to spread the word later, leaving you time for other pressing matters. It also ensures your tenants know where to turn for information and never feel that they've been left in the dark.

On the other side of the crisis coin is opportunity. When shit hits the fan, people begin to fail, and when that happens, opportunity arises. If you're just now trying to break into the rental game, at the precipice of disaster is where you may just get your big break.

Inevitably, there will be landlords that fold in the face of such difficulty because they failed to follow good business practices. Those folks would have done well to buy this book. Because they didn't take precautionary measures, they won't have the emergency funds needed to cover their expenses, and they won't have the wherewithal to find another way to pay them. They'll want to sell their rental units–and fast–so you'll be able to pressure them to get a good deal. It's supply and demand in action. This may seem a bit callous–benefiting from the foreclosures of other landlords, but you have to keep in mind that you didn't cause the foreclosure; you're simply helping to pick up the pieces. Take this opportunity to succeed where those before you did not.

The COVID-19 pandemic didn't fit the profile of most disasters, in which the course of events is pretty predictable: disaster hits, and tenants can't pay their rent, so landlords can't pay their mortgages. They foreclose. The pandemic surely sucked for everyone, but tenants had a bit of an advantage in this case because the government helped them with eviction moratoriums, while landlords left to foot the mortgage bill, and you can bet that the mortgage companies didn't let an unpaid bill fly.

The events of the past year did, however, help enforce the most basic principles of handling crises. Before you can even consider benefiting from one, you must know how to handle it and ensure your relationship with your tenants remains intact.

Being a landlord through the pandemic has been a serious struggle for countless people. Many I know had spent years building their businesses, barely breaking even. These folks lost it all in the last year.

It's never been more apparent how important it is to have an emergency fund available to face a situation like this. Those without one, both in business and personally, experienced the floor dropping out from under them this past year. You can't overestimate how useful it is to have cash on hand for bad situations.

Furthermore, as a landlord, you're the focal point for all of the anger, hatred, and panic that a crisis brings up in your tenants. If you have the nerve to ask for rent during hard times, your tenants will fault you and immediately go on the defensive. This is where empathy is paramount. Helping them to see your goal —maintaining their place of residence—as their own will help quite a bit.

When the pandemic hit, I immediately assessed the situation and determined where my business stood financially. I developed a plan and notified my tenants. Our shared goal, I explained to them, was to not lose anyone. Note the word choice here. I framed it as "lose" rather than "evict" because an eviction pits tenants against landlords. However, "lose" makes us a team. If one person is lost, we all hurt. In truth, this is a far more accurate description of the tenant-landlord relationship. If the tenants hurt, we as landlords hurt. Always remember that if you want to get the tenants to do what you want, then you need them on your team. This shared pursuit of a goal can- and often does- mean the difference between success and failure.

CONCLUSIONS

I would be a hypocrite if I didn't take this opportunity to acknowledge that I don't know everything. Clearly, this concise guide is no comprehensive instruction manual for being the ideal landlord. I certainly haven't gone over the ins and outs of every component of leadership or addressed every problem you'll ever encounter.

That was not the goal in writing this book. The goal was to provide the framework necessary to be more than a landlord or a property manager. I set out to show you what it takes to be a Property Leader.

With the concepts, tools, and action steps laid out in this guide, you are equipped to join a community of highly motivated and moral individuals who work to go beyond the bare minimum of landlording and achieve true Property Leading. These leaders unite their tenants under shared goals and lead everyone to success through deliberate and moral behavior.

You don't have to be a soldier, a born businessperson,

or a natural leader to thrive in the business of rental properties. If you remember, way back at the beginning of this book, I highlighted the fact that no one comes out of basic training a leader. Leadership isn't accomplished through a few months of basic training, but it's where the foundational tools are taught. The same is true for this book. I have provided the foundations required to be a true Property Leader. In applying these principles of consistency, knowledge, goal setting, learning from failure, and above all, remembering that leaders eat last, you will be prepared for whatever life throws at you, whether it's a whiny tenant or a global pandemic. Whatever the case, you will have what you need in order to be a prosperous Property Leader.

ABOUT THE AUTHOR

Anthony Russell is an Army veteran and Property Leader with the goal of helping others succeed as landlords His time as an Army Sergeant lead him to view property management with a strategic and militaristic eye. It is from this unique point of view that he teaches new and experienced landlords to embrace their leadership positions and improve the rental industry for everyone involved by becoming true Property Leaders.